The Holy Eucharist

ALTAR EDITION

Published by
THE CHURCH HYMNAL CORPORATION
800 Second Avenue • New York 10017

CERTIFICATE

I certify that this edition of
The Holy Eucharist
conforms to the text in Prayer Book Studies 21
as authorized for trial use
by the General Convention of 1970.

Charles Mortimer Guilbert
Custodian of the Standard Book of Common Prayer

Supplementary materials included
in this edition are from
Prayer Book Studies 19 and 22,
© 1970 by Charles Mortimer Guilbert

CONTENTS

Prefatory Note

This Altar book contains the eucharistic rites published in *Prayer Book Studies 21,* and authorized for trial use throughout the Church by the General Convention of 1970.

The main emphasis in the design of this book has been placed on the needs of the ministers at the Altar.[1] Consequently, this edition differs from the pew edition in the following respects:

1. The Offertory Sentences have been reprinted in the body of both the First and the Second Service;

2. The Proper Prefaces for each Service have been placed *in situ;*

3. Inconvenient page turns have been eliminated, as far as possible;

4. Musical settings for the Sursum Corda, the concluding doxology of the Great Thanksgiving, and the introduction to the Lord's Prayer have been included within the orders of service as a convenience;

5. The alternative procedure at the ministration of the Sacrament, found in the Additional Directions and Suggestions, has also been reprinted at the appropriate point in the First Service;

6. The Supplement includes the Exsultet noted for chant, for use at the Easter Vigil;

7. Two canticles from the Daily Office, suggested in *Prayer Book Studies 19* as suitable for use in the cele-

---

[1.] For this reason the Collects from the Proper of the Church Year (*Prayer Book Studies 19*) are not included in this book, it being assumed that the Proclamation of the Word of God will normally take place away from the Altar.

bration of the Holy Eucharist, will also be found in the Supplement.

8. Since the pagination of this book does not correspond to that of the pew edition, the page numbers of the latter are reproduced in brackets in the margin. This should facilitate the giving of directions, if necessary.

The musical settings of the Proper Prefaces and the Exsultet were prepared by the Joint Commission on Church Music. In setting the Prefaces, the Commission sought to find ways of adapting the ancient chant more closely to the natural patterns of English speech. Among the new principles it adopted is the avoidance of the *clivis* (descending two-note group) on unstressed syllables in the medial cadence. For purposes of trial use, two experimental forms of the chant were produced: one appears in the Prefaces for the First Service, and the other, somewhat more simplified and direct, in those for the Second Service. A simpler melody of the Sursum Corda was also produced, and appears on page 62.

The needs and convenience of the officiating ministers at the Altar have prompted the inclusion of 16 blank pages at the back of the book. They are punched and ready for insertion at any point in the Service. The pages may be used for special notes, reminders, alternative musical settings, and other pertinent materials.

It may be found helpful to attach tabs, easily available in stationery stores, to some of the most frequently used pages.

The format of this Altar edition is no less experimental than the format and typographic design of the various Prayer Book Studies and of the pew edition. It is hoped that after a suitable period, those who have used this book will send their comments and suggestions to the Standing Liturgical Commission, and thus assist it in devising improvements in format, lay-out, and style.

The Holy Eucharist

THE LITURGY FOR

THE PROCLAMATION OF

THE WORD OF GOD

AND CELEBRATION OF

THE HOLY COMMUNION

CONCERNING THE CELEBRATION

[38] The Holy Eucharist is the principal act of Christian worship on the Lord's Day.

At all celebrations of the Liturgy, it is fitting that the presiding Minister, whether bishop or priest, be assisted by other priests, and by deacons and lay persons.

When the Bishop is present, it is his prerogative as the chief sacramental minister of the Diocese to be the principal celebrant at the Lord's Table, and to preach the Gospel.

It is appropriate that other priests present stand with the presiding Minister at the altar, and join with him in the consecration of the gifts, in breaking the Bread, and in distributing Communion.

A deacon, when present, should read the Gospel and lead the prayer of Intercession. Deacons should also serve at the Lord's Table, preparing and placing on it the elements of bread and wine, and assisting in the ministration of the Sacrament to the People. In the absence of a deacon, his duties may be performed by an assisting priest.

Lay persons appointed by the presiding Minister should normally be assigned the reading of the Lessons which precede the Gospel; and in the absence of a deacon, they may lead the intercession.

The Order for Morning or Evening Prayer may be used in place of all that precedes the Offertory, provided that a Lesson from the Gospel is always included and that the Intercession conforms to the directions on page 111.

Additional Directions and Suggestions for the Ministers will be found on page 148.

THE HOLY EUCHARIST

First Service [39]

A Psalm, Hymn, or Anthem may be sung during the entrance of the Ministers.

The People being assembled, the Priest, standing, says ·

Almighty God, unto whom all hearts are open, all desires known, and from whom no secrets are hid: Cleanse the thoughts of our hearts by the inspiration of thy Holy Spirit, that we may perfectly love thee, and worthily magnify thy holy Name; through Christ our Lord. *Amen.*

Then the Ten Commandments (page 30) may be said, or the following:

Hear the words of our Lord Jesus Christ:

Thou shalt love the Lord thy God with all thy heart, and with all thy soul, and with all thy mind. This is the first and great commandment. And the second is like unto it; Thou shalt love thy neighbor as thyself. On these two commandments hang all the Law and the Prophets.

[40]   Here is sung or said

Lord, have mercy upon us.   Kyrie eleison.
Christ, have mercy upon us.   or   *Christe eleison.*
Lord, have mercy upon us.   Kyrie eleison.

or this

Holy God,
Holy and Mighty,
Holy Immortal One,
Have mercy upon us.

When appointed, the following Hymn or some other song of praise is sung or said, all standing

GLORY BE TO GOD ON HIGH,
  and on earth peace, good will towards men.
We praise thee, we bless thee,
  we worship thee,
  we glorify thee,
  we give thanks to thee for thy great glory,
O Lord God, heavenly King, God the Father Almighty.

O Lord, the only-begotten Son, Jesus Christ;
O Lord God, Lamb of God, Son of the Father,
  that takest away the sins of the world,
    have mercy upon us.
Thou that takest away the sins of the world,
  receive our prayer.
Thou that sittest at the right hand of God the Father,
  have mercy upon us.

For thou only art holy;
thou only art the Lord;
thou only, O Christ,
  with the Holy Ghost,
    art most high in the glory of God the Father. Amen.

THE PROCLAMATION OF THE WORD OF GOD

[41]

The presiding Minister says to the People

> **The Lord be with you.**
> Answer **And with thy spirit.**
> Priest **Let us pray.**

The Collect of the Day

The People respond Amen.

The Lessons

The People sit. One or two Lessons, as appointed, are announced and read. [See page 149 for forms for announcing and ending Epistles and other Lessons.]

A Psalm, Hymn, or Anthem may follow each Lesson.

Then, all standing, the Deacon or a priest reads the Gospel, first saying

THE HOLY GOSPEL of our Lord Jesus Christ according to _____.

The People respond **Glory be to thee, O Lord.**

At the end of the Gospel, the Deacon says

The Gospel of the Lord.

The People respond **Praise be to thee, O Christ.**

The Sermon

5

[42]   On Sundays and other festivals there follows, all standing

The Nicene Creed*

We believe in one God,
   the Father, the Almighty,
   maker of heaven and earth,
   of all that is seen and unseen.

We believe in one Lord, Jesus Christ,
   the only Son of God,
   eternally begotten of the Father,
   God from God, Light from Light,
   true God from true God,
   begotten, not made, one in Being with the Father.
   Through him all things were made.
For us men and for our salvation
   he came down from heaven:
by the power of the Holy Spirit
   he was born of the Virgin Mary, and became man.
For our sake he was crucified under Pontius Pilate;
   he suffered, died, and was buried.
   On the third day he rose again
     in fulfillment of the Scriptures;
   he ascended into heaven
     and is seated at the right hand of the Father.
He will come again in glory to judge the living and the
     dead,
   and his kingdom will have no end.

---

* This translation of the Creed has been adopted by the International Consultation on English Texts, ICET, and is recommended for experimental use in all Orders of the Eucharist.

We believe in the Holy Spirit, the Lord, the giver of life,   [43]
    who proceeds from the Father.
With the Father and the Son he is worshiped and
    glorified.
He has spoken through the Prophets.
We believe in one holy catholic and apostolic Church.
We acknowledge one baptism for the forgiveness of sins.
We look for the resurrection of the dead,
    and the life of the world to come. Amen.

The version of the Creed in the Book of Common Prayer may
be used in place of the preceding.

A confession of sin may be said here (page 9 or 36).

THE PRAYERS

Intercession is offered according to the following form, or
according to one of those provided on pages 111–130.

The Deacon, or some other person appointed, says

Let us pray for Christ's Church and the world.

After each paragraph of this prayer, the People may make an
appropriate response as directed by the Minister.

Almighty and everliving God, who hast taught us to make
prayers, and supplications, and to give thanks for all men:
Receive these our prayers which we offer unto thy Divine
Majesty, beseeching thee to inspire continually the Universal Church with the spirit of truth, unity, and concord;
and grant that all those who do confess thy holy Name
may agree in the truth of thy holy Word, and live in unity
and godly love.

[44] Give grace, O heavenly Father, to all Bishops and other Ministers, [especially _____], that they may, both by their life and doctrine, set forth thy true and lively Word, and rightly and duly administer thy holy Sacraments.

And to all thy People give thy heavenly grace; and especially to this congregation here present; that, with meek heart and due reverence, they may hear, and receive thy holy Word; truly serving thee in holiness and righteousness all the days of their life.

We beseech thee also, to rule the hearts of those who bear the authority of government in this and every land, [especially _____], and to lead them to wise decisions and right actions for the welfare of mankind, and for the peace of the world.

Grant to all people, Lord, the will and the wisdom to be good stewards of the riches of creation, that we neither selfishly waste nor wantonly destroy thy handiwork.

And we most humbly beseech thee, of thy goodness, O Lord, to comfort and succor all those who, in this transitory life, are in trouble, sorrow, need, sickness, or any other adversity, [especially _____].

And we also bless thy holy Name for all thy servants departed this life in thy faith and fear, [especially _____], beseeching thee to grant them continual growth in thy love and service, and to give us grace so to follow their good examples, that with them we may be partakers of thy heavenly kingdom.

Grant these our prayers, O Father, for Jesus Christ's sake, our only Mediator and Advocate. *Amen.*

If there is no celebration of the Communion, or if a priest is not available, the Service is concluded as directed on page 150.

Confession of Sin

The Deacon or Priest says the following, or the Exhortation on page 59. [The form given on page 36 may be used instead.]

Ye who do truly and earnestly repent you of your sins, and are in love and charity with your neighbors, and intend to lead the new life, following the commandments of God, and walking from henceforth in his holy ways; Draw near with faith, and make your humble confession to Almighty God, devoutly kneeling.

The People kneel. A period of silence may be kept; after which one of the Ministers leads the People in this General Confession:

Father almighty, Lord of heaven and earth:
We confess that we have sinned against thee
   in thought, word, and deed.
Have mercy upon us, O God,
   according to thy loving-kindness;
In thy great goodness,
   do away our offences,
   and cleanse us from our sins;
For Jesus Christ's sake. Amen.

or this

Almighty God, Father of our Lord Jesus Christ, Maker of all things, Judge of all men:

We acknowledge and bewail our manifold sins and wickedness, Which we, from time to time, most grievously have committed, By thought, word, and deed, against thy Divine Majesty, Provoking most justly thy wrath and indignation against us.

We do earnestly repent, And are heartily sorry for these our misdoings; The remembrance of them is grievous unto us; The burden of them is intolerable.

[46]   Have mercy upon us, Have mercy upon us, most merciful Father: for thy Son our Lord Jesus Christ's sake, Forgive us all that is past; And grant that we may ever hereafter, Serve and please thee in newness of life;

To the honor and glory of thy Name; Through Jesus Christ our Lord. Amen.

The Minister may then say

Hear the Word of God to all who truly turn to him:

Come unto me, all ye that travail and are heavy laden, and I will refresh you. [*St. Matthew 11:28*]

God so loved the world, that he gave his only-begotten Son, to the end that all that believe in him should not perish, but have everlasting life. [*St. John 3:16*]

This is a true saying, and worthy of all men to be received, That Christ Jesus came into the world to save sinners. [*1 Timothy 1:15*]

If any man sin, we have an Advocate with the Father, Jesus Christ the righteous; and he is the perfect offering for our sins, and not for ours only, but for the sins of the whole world. [*1 St. John 2:1-2*]

The Bishop, if he is present, or the Priest, stands and says this Absolution:

Almighty God, our heavenly Father, who of his great mercy hath promised forgiveness of sins to all those who with hearty repentance and true faith turn unto him; Have mercy upon you; pardon and deliver you from all your sins; confirm and strengthen you in all goodness; and bring you to everlasting life; through Jesus Christ our Lord. *Amen.*

The Peace

Here (or at one of the other places suggested on page 150), the Priest may say to the People

> **The Peace of the Lord be always with you.**
>
> Answer   **And with thy spirit.**

Then the Ministers and People may greet one another in the Name of the Lord.

THE CELEBRATION OF THE HOLY COMMUNION

The Priest, standing at the Holy Table, begins the Offertory with this or some other Sentence of Scripture:

Ascribe to the Lord the honor due his name; bring offerings and come into his courts. (*Psalm 96:8*)

The following Bidding may be used instead:

Let us with gladness present the offerings and oblations of our life and labor unto the Lord.

or one of these suggested Sentences:

Walk in love, as Christ loved us and gave himself for us, an offering and sacrifice to God. (*Ephesians 5:2*)

I pray you, brethren, by the mercies of God, to present yourselves as a living sacrifice, holy and acceptable to God, which is your spiritual worship. (*Romans 12:1*)

If you are offering your gift at the altar, and there remember that your brother has something against you, leave your gift there before the altar and go; first be reconciled to your brother, and then come and offer your gift. (*Matthew 5:23–24*)

Thine, O Lord, is the greatness, and the power, and the glory, and the victory, and the majesty. For all that is in the heaven and in the earth is thine. Thine is the kingdom, O Lord, and thou art exalted as head above all.
(*1 Chronicles 29:11*)

Worthy art thou, our Lord and God, to receive glory and honor and power; for thou hast created all things, and by thy will they exist and were created. (*Revelation 4:11*)

[47]   During the Offertory, a Psalm, Hymn, or Anthem may be sung.

Representatives of the Congregation bring the People's offerings of bread and wine, and money or other gifts, to the Deacon or Priest. The People stand while the offerings are presented and placed on the Altar.

The Great Thanksgiving

The People remain standing. The Priest faces them, and sings or says

> The Lord be with you.

People And with thy spirit.
Priest Lift up your hearts.
People We lift them up unto the Lord.
Priest Let us give thanks unto our Lord God.
People It is meet and right so to do.

Then, facing the Holy Table, the Priest proceeds [48]

It is very meet, right, and our bounden duty, that we should at all times, and in all places, give thanks unto thee, O Lord, Holy Father, Almighty, Everlasting God.

On all Sundays, and on other occasions when a Proper Preface is appointed, it is sung or said here.

Sursum Corda

The Lord be with you.

And with thy spir - it.

Lift up your hearts.

We lift them up un - to the Lord.

Let us give thanks un - to our Lord God.

It is meet and right so to do.

Proper Prefaces

[In the People's edition, the Proper Prefaces are printed as an appendix to the Services, beginning on page 115.]

Advent

From the First Sunday in Advent until Christmas Day, except on Saints' Days.

Because thou didst send thy well-beloved Son to redeem us from sin and death, and to make us, in him, sons and heirs of everlasting life: that when he shall come again in power and great triumph to judge the world, we may without shame or fear rejoice to behold his appearing:

Christmas

From Christmas Day until the Epiphany.

Because thou didst give Jesus Christ, thine only Son, to be born for us; who, by the mighty power of the Holy Spirit, was made perfect Man of the flesh of the Virgin Mary his mother: that we, being delivered from the bondage of sin, might receive power to become the sons of God:

Epiphany

From the Epiphany until Ash Wednesday, except on Saints' Days.

Through Jesus Christ our Lord; who, in the substance of our human nature, manifested his glory: that he might bring us out of darkness into his own marvelous light:

Incarnation

On the Feasts of the Presentation, Annunciation, Visitation, and Transfiguration.

Because in the Mystery of the Word made flesh, thou hast caused a new light to shine in our hearts, to give the knowledge of thy glory in the face of thy Son Jesus Christ our Lord:

Lent

From Ash Wednesday until Palm Sunday, except upon the Annunciation, and major Saints' Days.

Through Jesus Christ our Lord; who was in every way tempted as we are, yet did not sin; by whose grace we are able to triumph over every evil, and to live no longer unto ourselves, but unto him who died for us and rose again:

Therefore with Angels and Archangels, and with all the company of heaven, we laud and magnify thy glorious Name; evermore praising thee, and saying,

Priest and People

HOLY, HOLY, HOLY, Lord God of Hosts:
Heaven and earth are full of thy glory.
Glory be to thee, O Lord Most High.

Here may be added

Blessed is He that cometh in the Name of the Lord:
Hosanna in the highest!

The People may kneel.

Holy Week

From Palm Sunday through Maundy Thursday, and on Holy Cross Day.

Through Jesus Christ our Lord; who for our sins was lifted up upon the Cross, that he might draw all men to himself; who by his suffering and death became the way of eternal salvation to all who obey him:

Easter

From Easter Day until Ascension Day, except on major Holy Days.

But chiefly are we bound to praise thee for the glorious Resurrection of thy Son Jesus Christ our Lord, for he is the Paschal Lamb who by his death hath overcome death, and by his rising to life again hath opened to us the way of everlasting life:

Ascension

From Ascension Day until the Day of Pentecost, except on major Holy Days.

Through thy dearly beloved Son Jesus Christ our Lord; who, after his glorious Resurrection, openly appeared to all his Apostles, and in their sight was taken into heaven, to prepare a place for us: that where he is, there we might also be, and reign with him in glory:

Pentecost

On the day of Pentecost, and on the Feasts of the Apostles.

Through Jesus Christ our Lord; according to whose true promise the Holy Spirit came down from heaven upon the disciples, to teach them and to lead them into all truth; giving them boldness with fervent zeal to preach the Gospel to all nations:

Trinity Sunday

Whom with thy co-eternal Son and Holy Spirit we worship as one God, one Lord, in Trinity of Persons and in Unity of Being; and we celebrate the one and equal glory of thee, O Father, and of the Son, and of the Holy Spirit:

Therefore with Angels and Archangels, and with all the company of heaven, we laud and magnify thy glorious Name; evermore praising thee, and saying,

Priest and People

HOLY, HOLY, HOLY, Lord God of Hosts:
Heaven and earth are full of thy glory.
Glory be to thee, O Lord Most High.

Here may be added

Blessed is He that cometh in the Name of the Lord: Hosanna in the highest!

The People may kneel.

The Lord's Day

For use on the Sundays after Pentecost, but not on the succeeding weekdays.

Creator of the light and source of life; who hast made us in thine image and called us to new life in Jesus Christ our Lord:

or this

Through Jesus Christ our Lord, who on this day overcame death and the grave, and by his glorious resurrection opened to us the way of everlasting life:

or this

Who by water and the Holy Spirit hast made us a new people in Jesus Christ our Lord, to set forth thy glory in all the world:

All Saints

On All Saints' Day and upon certain other Saints' Days.

Who, in the multitude of thy saints, hast compassed us about with so great a cloud of witnesses: that we, rejoicing in their fellowship, may run with patience the race that is set before us; and, together with them, may receive the crown of glory that fadeth not away:

Apostles and Ordinations

On Feasts of the Apostles, and at the time of conferring Holy Orders.

Through the great Shepherd of thy flock, Jesus Christ our Lord; who after his Resurrection sent forth his Apostles to preach the Gospel, and to teach all nations; and promised to be with them always, even unto the end of the ages:

Baptism

For use at Baptism when there is no other Preface appointed.

Because in Jesus Christ our Lord thou hast received us as thy children, made us citizens of thy kingdom, and given us the Holy Spirit to guide us into all truth:

Marriage

Because thou hast ordained the solemn covenant of love between husband and wife as a witness of the union of thy son Jesus Christ with the holy fellowship of all faithful people:

Commemoration of the Dead

Through Jesus Christ our Lord; who brought to light the living hope of a blessed resurrection: that in our grief we may rejoice in full assurance of our change into the likeness of his glory:

Therefore with Angels and Archangels, and with all the company of heaven, we laud and magnify thy glorious Name; evermore praising thee, and saying,

[48]

Priest and People

HOLY, HOLY, HOLY, Lord God of Hosts:
Heaven and earth are full of thy glory.
Glory be to thee, O Lord Most High.

Here may be added

Blessed is He that cometh in the Name of the Lord:
Hosanna in the highest!

The People may kneel.

19

All glory be to thee, Almighty God, our heavenly Father, for that thou, of thy tender mercy, didst give thine only Son Jesus Christ to suffer death upon the Cross for our redemption; who made there, by his one oblation of himself once offered, a full, perfect, and sufficient sacrifice for the sins of the whole world; and did institute, and in his holy Gospel command us to continue, a perpetual memory of that his precious death and sacrifice, until his coming again:

At the following words concerning the Bread, the Priest is to hold it, or lay his hand upon it. And at the words concerning the Cup, he is to hold, or lay his hand upon, the Cup and any other vessel containing wine to be consecrated.

[49] For in the night in which he was betrayed, he took bread; and when he had given thanks, he brake it, and gave it to his disciples, saying, "Take, eat: This is my Body which is given for you. Do this in remembrance of me."

Likewise, after supper, he took the cup; and when he had given thanks, he gave it to them, saying, "Drink this, all of you: For this is my Blood of the New Covenant, which is shed for you, and for many, for the remission of sins. Do this, as oft as ye shall drink it, in remembrance of me."

Wherefore, O Lord and heavenly Father, we, thy humble servants, do celebrate and make here before thy Divine Majesty, with these thy holy Gifts, which we now offer unto thee, the memorial thy Son hath commanded us to make; having in remembrance his blessed passion and precious death, his mighty resurrection and glorious ascension; rendering unto thee most hearty thanks for the innumerable benefits procured unto us by the same.

And we most humbly beseech thee, O merciful Father, to hear us; and, of thy almighty goodness, vouchsafe to bless and sanctify, with thy Word and Holy Spirit, these Gifts of bread and wine; that we, receiving them according to thy Son our Savior Jesus Christ's holy institution, may be partakers of his most blessed Body and Blood.

And we earnestly desire thy fatherly goodness, mercifully to accept this our sacrifice of praise and thanksgiving; most humbly beseeching thee to grant that, by the merits and death of thy Son Jesus Christ, and through faith in his blood, we and all thy whole Church, may obtain remission of our sins, and all other benefits of his passion.

And here we offer and present unto thee, O Lord, our-selves, our souls and bodies, to be a reasonable, holy, and living sacrifice unto thee; humbly beseeching thee, that we, and all others who shall be partakers of this Holy Communion, may worthily receive the most precious Body and Blood of thy Son Jesus Christ, be filled with thy grace and heavenly benediction, and made one body with him, that he may dwell in us, and we in him. [50]

And although we are unworthy, through our manifold sins, to offer unto thee any sacrifice; yet we beseech thee to accept this our bounden duty and service; not weighing our merits, but pardoning our offences:

Through Jesus Christ our Lord; by whom, and with whom, in the unity of the Holy Ghost, all honor and glory be unto thee, O Father Almighty, world without end.

Amen.

And now, as our Savior Christ hath taught us, we are bold to say,

|Through Je-sus Christ our Lord; by whom, and with whom,

in the unity of the Holy Ghost, all honor and glo - ry be

un - to thee, O Fa-ther Al-migh-ty, world with-out end.

A-men.| And now, as our Sa-vior Christ hath taught us,

we are bold to say,

People and Priest

[50] Our Father, who art in heaven,
hallowed be thy Name,
thy kingdom come,
thy will be done,
on earth as it is in heaven.
Give us this day our daily bread.
And forgive us our trespasses,
as we forgive those who trespass against us.
And lead us not into temptation,
but deliver us from evil.

For thine is the kingdom, and the power, and the glory,
for ever and ever. Amen.

The Breaking of the Bread [51]

A period of silence is kept, during which the Priest breaks the consecrated Bread.

Then may be sung or said

(Alleluia.) Christ our Passover is sacrificed for us: *Therefore let us keep the feast.* (*Alleluia.*)

From Ash Wednesday until Easter Eve, Alleluia is omitted; and may be omitted at other times except during Easter Season.

The following prayer may be said:

We do not presume to come to this thy Table, O merciful Lord, trusting in our own righteousness, but in thy manifold and great mercies. We are not worthy so much as to gather up the crumbs under thy Table. But thou art the same Lord whose property is always to have mercy. Grant us therefore, gracious Lord, so to partake of the Body and Blood of thy dear Son Jesus Christ, that we may be cleansed from all our sins, and may evermore dwell in him, and he in us. *Amen.*

The Ministers receive the Sacrament in both kinds, and then immediately deliver it to the People.

The Bread and the Cup are given to the communicants with these words:

The Body of our Lord Jesus Christ, which was given for thee, preserve thy body and soul unto everlasting life. Take and eat this in remembrance that Christ died for thee, and feed on him in thy heart by faith, with thanksgiving.

The Blood of our Lord Jesus Christ, which was shed for thee, preserve thy body and soul unto everlasting life. Drink this in remembrance that Christ's Blood was shed for thee, and be thankful.

Or else, before receiving Communion himself, the Priest may say to the People:

> The Body and Blood of our Lord Jesus Christ, given for you, preserve your bodies and souls unto everlasting life. Take this in remembrance that Christ died for you, and feed on him in your hearts by faith, with thanksgiving.

The Gifts are then ministered with these words:

> The Body [Blood] of our Lord Jesus Christ. (*Amen.*)

Or he may use this Invitation:

> The Gifts of God for the People of God.

He may add:
> Take them in remembrance that Christ gives himself for you, and feed on him in your hearts by faith, with thanksgiving.

---

[52] During the ministration of Communion, Psalms, Hymns, or Anthems may be sung.

After Communion, the Priest says

Let us pray.

He then says this prayer. The People may repeat it with him.

Almighty and everliving God, we most heartily thank thee, For that thou dost feed us in these holy mysteries, With the spiritual food of the most precious Body and Blood of thy Son our Savior Jesus Christ:

And dost assure us thereby of thy favor and goodness toward us; And that we are very members incorporate in the mystical body of thy Son, The blessed company of all faithful people; And are also heirs, through hope, of thine everlasting kingdom.

And we humbly beseech thee, O heavenly Father, So to assist us with thy grace, That we may continue in that holy fellowship, And do all such good works as thou hast prepared for us to walk in:

Through Jesus Christ our Lord, To whom, with thee and the Holy Ghost, be all honor and glory, world without end. *Amen.*

The Bishop, if present, or the Priest, gives the blessing

The Peace of God, which passeth all understanding, keep your hearts and minds in the knowledge and love of God, and of his Son Jesus Christ our Lord: And the Blessing of God Almighty, the Father, the Son, and the Holy Ghost, be amongst you, and remain with you always. *Amen.*

or

[53]

The Blessing of God Almighty, the Father, the Son, and the Holy Spirit, be upon you, and remain with you for ever. *Amen.*

The Deacon (or Priest) may then dismiss the People

> Go forth into the world,
> rejoicing in the power of the Spirit.
> *Thanks be to God.*

or

> Go in peace to love and serve the Lord.
> *Thanks be to God.*

or

> Let us go forth in the Name of Christ.
> *Thanks be to God.*

OTHER FORMS OF
THE GREAT THANKSGIVING

which may be used in place of the Prayer in the preceding Rite.

[54]

I

[From the Liturgy of the Lord's Supper, 1967.]

After the Sursum Corda and Sanctus, the Priest continues

All glory be to thee, Almighty God, Holy Father, Creator of heaven and earth, who didst make us in thine own image: And when we had fallen into sin, thou of thy tender mercy didst give thine only-begotten Son Jesus Christ, to take our nature upon him, and to suffer death upon the Cross for our redemption: Who made there, by his one oblation of himself once offered, a full and perfect sacrifice for the whole world; And instituted and commanded us to continue this perpetual memorial of his precious death and sacrifice, until his coming again.

At the following words concerning the Bread, the Priest is to hold it, or lay his hand upon it. And at the words concerning the Cup, he is to hold, or lay his hand upon, the Cup and any other vessel containing wine to be consecrated.

For in the night in which he was betrayed, he took bread; and when he had given thanks to thee, he broke it, and gave it to his disciples, and said, "Take, eat: This is my Body which is given for you. Do this in remembrance of me."

In the same way also, after supper, he took the cup; and when he had given thanks, he gave it to them and said, "Drink this, all of you: For this is my Blood of the New Covenant, which is poured out for you and many for the forgiveness of sins. Do this, as often as you drink it, in remembrance of me."

26

Wherefore, O Lord and Holy Father, we thy people do [55] celebrate here before thy Divine Majesty, with these thy holy Gifts, which we offer unto thee, the memorial of the blessed Passion and precious Death of thy dear Son, his mighty Resurrection and glorious Ascension, looking for his Coming again in power and great glory. And herewith we offer and present unto thee, O Lord, ourselves, which is our bounden duty and service. And we entirely desire thy fatherly goodness mercifully to accept, through the eternal mediation of our Savior Jesus Christ, this our sacrifice of praise and thanksgiving.

We pray thee, gracious Father, of thine almighty power, to bless and sanctify us and these holy Mysteries with thy Life-giving Word and Holy Spirit. Fill with thy grace all who partake of the Body and Blood of our Lord Jesus Christ. Make us one Body, that he may dwell in us and we in him. And grant that with boldness we may confess thy Name in constancy of faith, and at the last Day enter with all thy saints into the joy of thine eternal kingdom:

Through the same Jesus Christ our Lord; by whom, and with whom, and in whom, in the unity of the Holy Spirit all honor and glory be unto thee, O Father Almighty, world without end.

Amen.

And now, as our Savior Christ hath taught us, we are bold to say,

[55]

II

After the Sursum Corda and Sanctus, the Priest continues

All glory be to thee, Almighty God, our heavenly Father, for that thou, of thy tender mercy, didst give thine only Son Jesus Christ to suffer death upon the Cross for our redemption; who made there by his one oblation of himself once offered, a full, perfect, and sufficient sacrifice for [56] the sins of the whole world; and did institute, and in his holy Gospel command us to continue, a perpetual memory of that his precious death and sacrifice, until his coming again.

At the following words concerning the Bread, the Priest is to hold it, or lay his hand upon it. And at the words concerning the Cup, he is to hold, or lay his hand upon, the Cup and any other vessel containing wine to be consecrated.

For in the night in which he was betrayed, he took bread; and when he had given thanks, he brake it, and gave it to his disciples, saying, "Take, eat: This is my Body, which is given for you. Do this in remembrance of me."

Likewise, after supper, he took the cup; and when he had given thanks, he gave it to them, saying, "Drink this, all of you: For this is my Blood of the New Covenant, which is shed for you, and for many, for the remission of sins. Do this, as oft as ye shall drink it in remembrance of me."

Wherefore, O Lord and heavenly Father, we, thy humble servants, do celebrate and make here before thy Divine Majesty, with these thy holy Gifts, which we now offer unto thee, the memorial thy Son hath commanded us to make; having in remembrance his blessed passion and precious death, his mighty resurrection and glorious ascension; rendering unto thee most hearty thanks for the innumerable benefits procured unto us by the same.

And we most humbly beseech thee, O merciful Father, to hear us; and, of thy almighty goodness, vouchsafe to bless and sanctify, with thy Word and Holy Spirit, these Gifts of bread and wine; that we, receiving them according to thy Son our Savior Jesus Christ's holy institution, may be partakers of his most blessed Body and Blood.

And we earnestly desire thy fatherly goodness, mercifully to accept this our sacrifice of praise and thanksgiving; and to accept us, our souls and bodies, in union with our Savior Jesus Christ, a reasonable, holy, and living sacrifice unto thee; beseeching thee to make us one body with him, that he may dwell in us, and we in him:

[57]

Through Jesus Christ our Lord; by whom, and with whom, in the unity of the Holy Ghost, all honor and glory be unto thee, O Father Almighty, world without end.

Amen.

And now, as our Savior Christ hath taught us, we are bold to say,

29

[57] THE DECALOGUE

The Ten Commandments with their responses may be substituted for the Summary of the Law, or may precede it, the People kneeling.

God spake these words, and said:
I am the Lord thy God; Thou shalt have none other gods but me.
Lord, have mercy upon us, and incline our hearts to keep this law.

Thou shalt not make to thyself any graven image, nor the likeness of any thing that is in heaven above, or in the earth beneath, or in the water under the earth; thou shalt not bow down to them, nor worship them.
Lord, have mercy upon us, and incline our hearts to keep this law.

Thou shalt not take the Name of the Lord God in vain.
Lord, have mercy upon us, and incline our hearts to keep this law.

[58] Remember that thou keep holy the Sabbath-day.
Lord, have mercy upon us, and incline our hearts to keep this law.

Honor thy father and thy mother.
Lord, have mercy upon us, and incline our hearts to keep this law.

Thou shalt do no murder.
Lord, have mercy upon us, and incline our hearts to keep this law.

Thou shalt not commit adultery.
Lord, have mercy upon us, and incline our hearts to keep this law.

Thou shalt not steal.
Lord, have mercy upon us, and incline our hearts to keep this law.

Thou shalt not bear false witness against thy neighbor.
Lord, have mercy upon us, and incline our hearts to keep this law.

Thou shalt not covet.
Lord, have mercy upon us, and incline our hearts to keep this law.

The Minister may then proceed directly to the Hymn, "Glory be to God on High", or to the Salutation and Collect of the Day.

[59] AN EXHORTATION

Beloved in the Lord:

Our Savior Christ, on the night before he suffered, established the Sacrament of his Body and Blood: as a sign and pledge of his love, for the continual remembrance of the sacrifice of his death, and for a spiritual sharing in his life. For in those holy Mysteries we are made one with Christ, and Christ with us; we are made one body in him, and fellow-members one of another.

Having in mind, therefore, his great love for us, and in obedience to his command, his Church renders to Almighty God our heavenly Father never-ending thanks:

for the creation of the world,
for his continual providence over us,
for his love for all mankind, and
for the redemption of the world by our Savior Christ, who took upon himself our flesh, and humbled himself even to death on the Cross, that he might make us the children of God by the power of the Holy Spirit, and exalt us to everlasting life.

But if we are to share rightly in the celebration of those holy Mysteries, and be nourished by that spiritual Food, we must remember the dignity of that holy Sacrament. I therefore call upon you to consider how Saint Paul exhorts all persons to prepare themselves carefully before eating of that Bread and drinking of that Cup.

For as the benefit is great, if with penitent hearts and [60] living faith we receive the holy Sacrament; so is the danger great, if we receive it improperly, not recognizing the Lord's Body. Judge yourselves therefore, my brothers, lest you be judged by the Lord.

Examine your lives and conduct by the rule of God's commandments, that you may perceive wherein you have offended in what you have done or left undone, whether in thought, word, or deed. And acknowledge your sins before Almighty God, with full purpose of amendment of life, being ready to make restitution for all injuries and wrongs done by you to others; and also being ready to forgive those who have offended you, in order that you yourselves may be forgiven. And then, being reconciled with your brothers, come to the banquet of that most heavenly Food.

And if in your own preparation, you cannot quiet your conscience, but need help and counsel, then go to a discreet and understanding Priest, and open your grief to him: that you may receive the benefit of Absolution and spiritual counsel and advice; to the removal of scruple and doubt, the assurance of pardon, and the strengthening of your faith.

To Christ our Lord who loves us, and washed us in his own blood, and made us a kingdom of priests to serve his God and Father: to him be glory in the Church evermore. Through him let us offer continually the sacrifice of praise which is our bounden duty and service, and, with faith in him, come boldly before the Throne of grace [and humbly confess our sins to Almighty God].

A PENITENTIAL ORDER [61]

This Order may be used immediately before the Liturgy (in which case the Collect for Purity is to be omitted), or as a separate service.

When used separately, a Sermon or the Exhortation on page 32 may follow the Sentences; and then, after the confession of sin, the service may be concluded with suitable prayers, and the Grace.

The Minister begins with this Sentence:

Grace to you and peace from God our Father and the Lord Jesus Christ. [*Philippians 1:2*]

He then adds one or more of the following:

If we say that we have no sin, we deceive ourselves, and the truth is not in us. But if we confess our sins, God, who is faithful and just, will forgive our sins and cleanse us from all unrighteousness. [*1 John 1:8–9*]

Since we have a great high priest who has passed through the heavens, Jesus, the Son of God, let us with confidence draw near to the throne of grace, that we may receive mercy and find grace to help in time of need.
[*Hebrews 4:14*]

Jesus said,
The first commandment is this: "Hear, O Israel: The Lord your God is the only Lord. Love the Lord your God with all your heart, with all your soul, with all your mind, and with all your strength."
The second is this: "Love your neighbor as yourself." There is no other commandment greater than these.
[*Mark 12:29–31*]

Then follows a confession of sin.

[62] Confession of Sin

[For use with the First Service]

The Minister says

Let us confess our sins against God and our neighbor.

A period of silence may be observed.

Minister and People

Most merciful God,
we confess that we have sinned against thee
in thought, word and deed:
we have not loved thee with our whole heart;
we have not loved our neighbors as ourselves.
We pray thee of thy mercy
   forgive what we have been,
   amend what we are,
   direct what we shall be;
that we may delight in thy will,
and walk in thy ways,
through Jesus Christ our Lord. Amen.

or

Father almighty, Lord of heaven and earth:
We confess that we have sinned against thee
   in thought, word, and deed.
Have mercy upon us, O God,
   according to thy loving-kindness;
In thy great goodness,
   do away our offences,
   and cleanse us from our sins;
for Jesus Christ's sake. Amen.

The Bishop, if present, or the Priest stands and says

The Almighty and merciful Lord grant you Absolution and Remission of all your sins, true repentance, amendment of life, and the grace and consolation of his Holy Spirit. *Amen.*

[63]

Confession of Sin

[For use with the Second Service]

The Minister says

Let us confess our sins against God and our neighbor.

A period of silence may be observed.

Minister and People

Most merciful God,
we confess that we have sinned against you
in thought, word and deed:
we have not loved you with our whole heart;
we have not loved our neighbors as ourselves.
We pray you of your mercy
    forgive what we have been,
    amend what we are,
    direct what we shall be;
that we may delight in your will,
and walk in your ways,
through Jesus Christ our Lord. Amen.

The Bishop, if present, or the Priest stands and says

Almighty God have mercy on you, forgive you all your sins, through our Lord Jesus Christ; strengthen you in all goodness, and by the power of the Holy Spirit, keep you in eternal life. *Amen.*

[64] CONCERNING THE CELEBRATION

The Holy Eucharist is the principal act of Christian worship on the Lord's Day.

At all celebrations of the Liturgy, it is fitting that the presiding Minister, whether bishop or priest, be assisted by other priests, and by deacons and lay persons.

When the Bishop is present, it is his prerogative as the chief sacramental minister of the Diocese to be the principal celebrant at the Lord's Table, and to preach the Gospel.

It is appropriate that other priests present stand with the presiding Minister at the altar, and join with him in the consecration of the gifts, in breaking the Bread, and in distributing Communion.

A deacon, when present, should read the Gospel and lead the Prayer of Intercession. Deacons should also serve at the Lord's Table, preparing and placing on it the elements of bread and wine, and assisting in the ministration of the Sacrament to the People. In the absence of a deacon, his duties may be performed by an assisting priest.

Lay persons appointed by the presiding Minister should normally be assigned the reading of the Lessons which precede the Gospel; and in the absence of a deacon, they may lead the intercession.

The Order for Morning or Evening Prayer may be used in place of all that precedes the Offertory, provided that a Lesson from the Gospel is always included and that the Intercession conforms to the directions on page 111.

Additional Directions and Suggestions for the Ministers will be found on page 148.

THE HOLY EUCHARIST

Second Service

[65]

A Psalm, Hymn, or Anthem may be sung during the entrance of the Ministers.

The People being assembled, and all standing, the Priest says

Blessed be God: Father, Son, and Holy Spirit.

People

And blessed be his Kingdom, now and for ever. Amen.

From Easter Day through the Day of Pentecost, in place of the above, he says

    Alleluia! Christ is risen.
People **The Lord is risen indeed. Alleluia!**

The Priest may say

Almighty God, to you all hearts are open, all desires known, and from you no secrets are hid: Cleanse the thoughts of our hearts by the inspiration of your Holy Spirit, that we may perfectly love you, and worthily magnify your holy Name; through Christ our Lord. *Amen.*

[66] When appointed, the following Hymn* or some other song of praise is sung or said, all standing

GLORY TO GOD IN THE HIGHEST,
   and peace to his people on earth.
Lord God, heavenly King,
almighty God and Father,
      we worship you, we give you thanks,
      we praise you for your glory.
Lord Jesus Christ, only Son of the Father,
Lord God, Lamb of God,
you take away the sin of the world:
      have mercy on us;
you are seated at the right hand of the Father:
      receive our prayer.
For you alone are the Holy One,
you alone are the Lord,
you alone are the Most High,
      Jesus Christ,
      with the Holy Spirit,
      in the glory of God the Father. Amen.

On other occasions the following is used

Lord, have mercy.   Kyrie eleison.
Christ, have mercy.   or   *Christe eleison.*
Lord, have mercy.   Kyrie eleison.

or this

Holy God,
Holy and Mighty,
Holy Immortal One,
Have mercy upon us.

* An ICET text.

40

THE PROCLAMATION OF THE WORD OF GOD

The presiding Minister says to the People

The Lord be with you.
Answer   **And also with you.**
Priest   **Let us pray.**

The Collect of the Day

The People respond Amen.

The Lessons

The People sit. One or two Lessons, as appointed, are announced and read. [See page 149 for forms for announcing and ending Epistles and other Lessons.]

A Psalm, Hymn, or Anthem may follow each Lesson.

Then, all standing, the Deacon or a priest reads the Gospel, first saying

THE HOLY GOSPEL of our Lord Jesus Christ according to _____.

The People respond   **Glory to you, Lord Christ.**

At the end of the Gospel, the Deacon says

The Gospel of the Lord.

The People respond   **Praise to you, Lord Christ.**

The Sermon

41

[68]
On Sundays and other festivals there follows, all standing

The Nicene Creed

We believe in one God,
  the Father, the Almighty,
  maker of heaven and earth,
  of all that is seen and unseen.

We believe in one Lord, Jesus Christ,
  the only Son of God,
  eternally begotten of the Father,
  God from God, Light from Light,
  true God from true God,
  begotten, not made, one in Being with the Father.
  Through him all things were made.
  For us men and for our salvation
    he came down from heaven:
  by the power of the Holy Spirit
    he was born of the Virgin Mary, and became man.
  For our sake he was crucified under Pontius Pilate;
    he suffered, died, and was buried.
    On the third day he rose again
      in fulfillment of the Scriptures;
    he ascended into heaven
      and is seated at the right hand of the Father.
  He will come again in glory to judge the living and the
    dead,
  and his kingdom will have no end.

We believe in the Holy Spirit, the Lord, the giver of life,
  who proceeds from the Father.
  With the Father and the Son he is worshiped and
    glorified.
  He has spoken through the Prophets.

We believe in one holy catholic and apostolic Church. [69]
We acknowledge one baptism for the forgiveness of sins.
We look for the resurrection of the dead,
   and the life of the world to come. Amen.

A confession of sin may be said here, or after the Intercession.

Confession of Sin

The Minister says

Let us confess our sins against God and our neighbor.

A period of silence may be observed.

Minister and People

Most merciful God,
we confess that we have sinned against you
in thought, word and deed:
we have not loved you with our whole heart;
we have not loved our neighbors as ourselves.
We pray you of your mercy
   forgive what we have been,
   amend what we are,
   direct what we shall be;
that we may delight in your will,
and walk in your ways,
   through Jesus Christ our Lord. Amen.

The Bishop, if present, or the Priest stands and says

Almighty God have mercy on you, forgive you all your sins, through our Lord Jesus Christ; strengthen you in all goodness, and by the power of the Holy Spirit, keep you in eternal life. *Amen.*

[70] # THE PRAYERS

Here Prayer is offered with intercession for

The Universal Church and all its members

The Nation and all in authority

The welfare of the world

The concerns of the local community

Those who suffer and those in any trouble

The departed (with commemoration of a saint when appropriate)

See pages 111–130 for various forms of Intercession.

The Peace

Here (or at one of the other places suggested on page 150), the Priest may say to the People

The Peace of the Lord be always with you.

Answer **And also with you.**

Then the Ministers and People may greet one another in the Name of the Lord.

If there is no celebration of the Communion, or if a priest is not available, the Service is concluded as directed on page 150.

THE CELEBRATION OF THE HOLY COMMUNION

The Priest, standing at the Holy Table, begins the Offertory with this or some other Sentence of Scripture:

Ascribe to the Lord the honor due his Name; bring offerings and come into his courts. [*Psalm 96:8*]

44

The following Bidding may be used instead:

Let us with gladness present the offerings and oblations of our life and labor unto the Lord.

or one of these suggested Sentences:

Walk in love, as Christ loved us and gave himself for us, an offering and sacrifice to God. (*Ephesians 5:2*)

I pray you, brethren, by the mercies of God, to present yourselves as a living sacrifice, holy and acceptable to God, which is your spiritual worship. (*Romans 12:1*)

If you are offering your gift at the altar, and there remember that your brother has something against you, leave your gift there before the altar and go; first be reconciled to your brother, and then come and offer your gift. (*Matthew 5:23–24*)

Yours, O Lord, is the greatness, the power, the glory, the victory, and the majesty. For everything in the heaven and on earth is yours. Yours, O Lord, is the kingdom, and you are exalted as head over all. (*1 Chronicles 29:11*)

O Lord our God: you are worthy to receive glory and honor and power; because you have created all things; and by your will they were created and have their being. (*Revelation 4:11*)

During the Offertory, a Psalm, Hymn, or Anthem may be sung.

[71]   Representatives of the Congregation bring the People's offerings of bread and wine, and money or other gifts, to the Deacon or Priest. The People stand while the offerings are presented and placed on the Altar.

The Great Thanksgiving

The People remain standing. The Priest faces them, and sings or says

Priest   The Lord be with you.
People   And also with you.
Priest   Lift up your hearts.
People   We lift them up to the Lord.
Priest   Let us give thanks to the Lord our God.
People   It is right to give him thanks and praise.

Then, facing the Holy Table, the Priest proceeds

It is right, and a good and joyful thing, always and everywhere to give thanks to you, Father Almighty, Creator of heaven and earth:

On all Sundays, and on other occasions when a Proper Preface is appointed, it is sung or said here.

Therefore we praise you,
joining our voices with angels and archangels
and with all the company of heaven,
who for ever sing this hymn
to proclaim the glory of your Name:

Priest and People

Holy, holy, holy Lord, God of power and might,
heaven and earth are full of your glory.
   Hosanna in the highest.
Blessed is he who comes in the name of the Lord.
   Hosanna in the highest.

Sursum Corda

[Other melodies for the Sursum Corda will be found on page 62.]

[114]

The Lord be with you.

And al-so with you.

Lift up your hearts.

We lift them up to the Lord.

Let us give thanks to the Lord our God.

or

Let us give thanks to the Lord our God.

It is right to give him thanks and praise.

47

Proper Prefaces

[In the People's edition, the Proper Prefaces are printed as an appendix to the Services, beginning on page 115.]

Advent

From the First Sunday in Advent until Christmas Day, except on Saints' Days.

Because you sent your well-beloved Son to redeem us from sin and death, and to make us, in him, sons and heirs of everlasting life: that when he shall come again in power and great triumph to judgge the world, we may without shame or fear rejoice to behold his appearing:

Christmas

From Christmas Day until the Epiphany.

Because you gave Jesus Christ, your only Son, to be born for us; who, by the mighty power of the Holy Spirit, was made perfect Man of the flesh of the Virgin Mary his mother: that we, being delivered from the bondage of sin, might receive power to become the sons of God:

Epiphany

From the Epiphany until Ash Wednesday, except on Saints' Days.

Through Jesus Christ our Lord; who, in the substance of our human nature, manifested his glory: that he might bring us out of darkness into his own marvelous light:

Incarnation

On the Feasts of the Presentation, Annunciation, Visitation, and Transfiguration.

Because in the Mystery of the Word made flesh, you have caused a new light to shine in our hearts, to give the knowledge of your glory in the face of your Son Jesus Christ our Lord:

Lent

From Ash Wednesday until Palm Sunday, except upon the Annunciation, and major Saints' Days.

Through Jesus Christ our Lord; who was in every way tempted as we are, yet did not sin; by whose grace we are able to triumph over every evil, and to live no longer unto ourselves, but unto him who died for us and rose again:

Therefore we praise you,
joining our voices with angels and archangels
and with all the company of heaven,
who for ever sing this hymn
to proclaim the glory of your Name:

Priest and People

Holy, holy, holy Lord, God of power and might,
heaven and earth are full of your glory.
    Hosanna in the highest.
Blessed is he who comes in the name of the Lord.
    Hosanna in the highest.

Holy Week

From Palm Sunday through Maundy Thursday, and on Holy Cross Day.

Through Jesus Christ our Lord; who for our sins was lifted up upon the Cross, that he might draw all men to himself; who by his suffering and death became the way of eternal salvation to all who obey him:

Easter

From Easter Day until Ascension Day, except on major Holy Days.

But chiefly are we bound to praise you for the glorious Resurrection of your Son Jesus Christ our Lord, for he is the Paschal Lamb who by his death has overcome death, and by his rising to life again has opened to us the way of everlasting life:

Ascension

From Ascension Day until the Day of Pentecost, except on major Holy Days.

Through your dearly beloved Son Jesus Christ our Lord; who, after his glorious Resurrection, openly appeared to all his Apostles, and in their sight was taken into heaven, to prepare a place for us: that where he is, there we might also be, and reign with him in glory:

Pentecost

On the day of Pentecost, and on the Feasts of the Apostles.

Through Jesus Christ our Lord; according to whose true promise the Holy Spirit came down from heaven upon the disciples, to teach them and to lead them into all truth; giving them boldness with fervent zeal to preach the Gospel to all nations:

Trinity Sunday

Whom with your co-eternal Son and Holy Spirit we worship as one God, one Lord, in Trinity of Persons and in Unity of Being; and we celebrate the one and equal glory, O Father, of you, and of the Son, and of the Holy Spirit:

———————

Therefore we praise you,
joining our voices with angels and archangels
and with all the company of heaven,
who for ever sing this hymn
to proclaim the glory of your Name:

Priest and People

Holy, holy, holy Lord, God of power and might,
heaven and earth are full of your glory.
    Hosanna in the highest.
Blessed is he who comes in the name of the Lord.
    Hosanna in the highest.

The Lord's Day

For use on the Sundays after Pentecost, but not on the succeeding weekdays.

For you are the source of light and life; you made us in your image and called us to new life in Jesus Christ our Lord:

or this

Through Jesus Christ our Lord, who on this day overcame death and the grave, and by his glorious resurrection opened to us the way of everlasting life:

or this

For by water and the Holy Spirit you have made us a new people in Jesus Christ our Lord, to set forth your glory in all the world:

All Saints

On All Saints' Day and upon certain other Saints' Days.

For in the multitude of your saints, you have compassed us about with so great a cloud of witnesses: that we, rejoicing in their fellowship, may run with patience the race that is set before us; and, together with them, may receive the crown of glory that never fades away:

Apostles and Ordinations

On Feasts of the Apostles, and at the time of conferring Holy Orders.

Through the great Shepherd of your flock, Jesus Christ our Lord; who after his Resurrection sent forth his Apostles to preach the Gospel, and to teach all nations; and promised to be with them always, even unto the end of the ages:

Baptism

For use at Baptism when there is no other Preface appointed.

Because in Jesus Christ our Lord you have received us as your children, made us citizens of your kingdom, and given us the Holy Spirit to guide us into all truth:

Marriage

Because you have ordained the solemn covenant of love between husband and wife as a witness of the union of your son Jesus Christ with the holy fellowship of all faithful people:

Commemoration of the Dead

Through Jesus Christ our Lord; who brought to light the living hope of a blessed resurrection: that in our grief we may rejoice in full assurance of our change into the likeness of his glory:

---

[71]

Therefore we praise you,
joining our voices with angels and archangels
and with all the company of heaven,
who for ever sing this hymn
to proclaim the glory of your Name:

Priest and People

Holy, holy, holy Lord, God of power and might,
heaven and earth are full of your glory.
Hosanna in the highest.
Blessed is he who comes in the name of the Lord.
Hosanna in the highest.

[72]
The People may kneel.

Then the Priest continues

Holy and gracious Father,
in your infinite love you made us for yourself;
and when we fell into sin
and became subject to evil and death,
you, in your mercy, sent Jesus Christ,
your only and eternal Son,
to share our human nature,
to live and die as one of us
to reconcile us to you,
the God and Father of all.

He stretched out his arms upon the Cross,
and offered himself, in obedience to your will,
a perfect sacrifice for all mankind.

At the following words concerning the Bread, the Priest is to
hold it, or lay his hand upon it. And at the words concerning
the Cup, he is to hold, or lay his hand upon, the Cup and any
other vessel containing wine to be consecrated.

On the night he was handed over to suffering and death,
our Lord Jesus Christ took bread;
and when he had given thanks to you,
he broke it, and gave it to his disciples,
and said, "Take this and eat it:
This is my Body, which is given for you.
Do this for the remembrance of me."

After supper he took the cup of wine;
and when he had given thanks, he gave it to them,
and said, "Drink this, all of you:

This is my Blood of the new Covenant, [73]
which is shed for you and for many
for the forgiveness of sins.
Whenever you drink it, do this for the remembrance of
   me."

Priest and People

   Christ has died,
   Christ is risen,
   Christ will come again.

The Priest continues

We celebrate the memorial of our redemption, O Father,
in this sacrifice of praise and thanksgiving,
and we offer you these Gifts.
Sanctify them by your Holy Spirit
to be for your people the Body and Blood of your Son,
the holy food and drink of new and unending life in him.
Sanctify us also
that we may faithfully receive this holy Sacrament,
and serve you in unity, constancy, and peace;
and at the last day bring us with all your saints
into the joy of your eternal kingdom.

All this we ask through your Son Jesus Christ:
By him, and with him, and in him,
in the unity of the Holy Spirit
all honor and glory is yours, Almighty Father,
now and for ever.

Amen.

As our Savior Christ has taught us, we now pray,

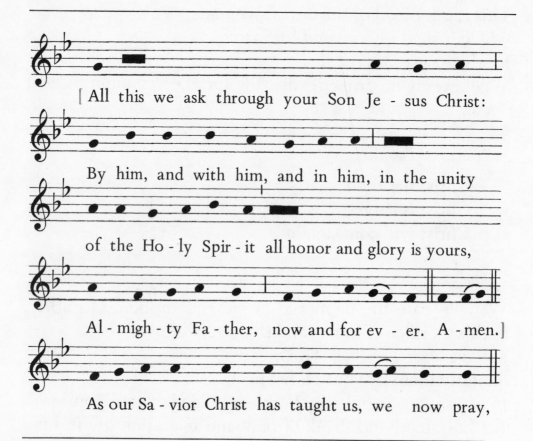

[All this we ask through your Son Je - sus Christ:

By him, and with him, and in him, in the unity

of the Ho - ly Spir - it all honor and glory is yours,

Al - migh - ty Fa - ther, now and for ev - er. A - men.]

As our Sa - vior Christ has taught us, we now pray,

[74]   People and Priest

Our Father in heaven,
    holy be your Name,
    your kingdom come,
    your will be done,
        on earth as in heaven.
Give us today our daily bread.
Forgive us our sins
    as we forgive those who sin against us.
Do not bring us to the test
    but deliver us from evil.

For the kingdom, the power, and the glory are yours
    now and for ever. Amen.

The Breaking of the Bread

A period of silence is kept, during which the Priest breaks the consecrated Bread.

Then may be sung or said

(Alleluia.) Christ our Passover is sacrificed for us:
Therefore let us keep the feast. (*Alleluia.*)

From Ash Wednesday until Easter Eve, Alleluia is omitted; and may be omitted at other times except during Easter Season.

Facing the People, the Priest says the following Sentence of Invitation:

The Gifts of God for the People of God.

He may add: Take them in remembrance that Christ gives himself for you, and feed on him in your hearts by faith, with thanksgiving.

The Ministers receive the Sacrament in both kinds, and then immediately deliver it to the People.

[75]

The Bread and the Cup are given with these words, to which the communicant may respond, *Amen.*

The Body [Blood] of our Lord Jesus Christ keep you in everlasting life.

or this

The Body of Christ, the Bread of heaven.
The Blood of Christ, the Cup of salvation.

During the ministration of Communion, Psalms, Hymns, or Anthems may be sung.

[75]   After Communion, the Priest says

Let us pray.

People and Priest

**Eternal God, Heavenly Father,
you have accepted us as living members of your Son
     our Savior Jesus Christ,
and you have fed us with spiritual food
     in the Sacrament of his Body and Blood.
Send us now into the world in peace,
     and grant us strength and courage
     to love and serve you
     with gladness and singleness of heart. Amen.**

or this

**Almighty and everliving God,
you have fed us with the spiritual food
     of the most precious Body and Blood
     of your Son, our Savior Jesus Christ;**

[76]   **You have assured us, in these holy Mysteries,
     that we are living members
     of the Body of your Son,
     and heirs of your eternal kingdom.**

**And now, Father, send us out
     to do the work you have given us to do,
To love and serve you
     as faithful witnesses of Christ our Lord.**

**To him, to you, and to the Holy Spirit,
     be honor and glory now and for ever. Amen.**

The Bishop, if present, or the Priest, may bless the People.

The Deacon (or Priest) may dismiss them with these words:

Go forth into the world,
rejoicing in the power of the Spirit.
Thanks be to God.

or

Go in peace to love and serve the Lord.
Thanks be to God.

or

Let us go forth in the Name of Christ.
Thanks be to God.

[77] ANOTHER FORM OF THE GREAT THANKSGIVING

[Based on the Liturgy of the Lord's Supper, 1967]

After the Sursum Corda and the Sanctus, the Priest continues

All glory is yours, Almighty God, Holy Father:
You made us in your own image;
and when we had fallen into sin,
you gave your only-begotten Son Jesus Christ,
to take our nature upon him,
and to suffer death upon the Cross for our redemption.
He made there, by his one oblation of himself,
a full and perfect sacrifice for the whole world;
And instituted and commanded us to continue
this memorial of his precious death and sacrifice,
until his coming again.

At the following words concerning the Bread, the Priest is to
hold it, or lay his hand upon it. And at the words concerning
the Cup, he is to hold, or lay his hand upon, the Cup and any
other vessel containing wine to be consecrated.

For in the night in which he was betrayed, he took bread;
and when he had given thanks to you,
he broke it, and gave it to his disciples, and said,
"Take, eat: This is my Body which is given for you.
Do this in remembrance of me."

After supper, he took the cup;
and when he had given thanks, he gave it to them and said,
"Drink this, all of you: For this is my Blood of the New
  Covenant
which is poured out for you and for many
for the forgiveness of sins.
Do this, as often as you drink it, in remembrance of me."

60

Therefore, O Lord and Holy Father, we your people [78]
celebrate here before your Divine Majesty,
with these holy Gifts which we offer to you,
the memorial of the blessed Passion
and precious Death of your dear Son,
his mighty Resurrection and glorious Ascension,
looking for his Coming again in power and great glory.
And with these Gifts, O Lord, we offer to you ourselves,
for this is our duty and service.
And we pray you, in your goodness and mercy, to accept,
through the eternal mediation of our Savior Jesus Christ,
this our sacrifice of praise and thanksgiving.

Gracious Father, in your almighty power,
bless and sanctify us and these holy Mysteries
with your Life-giving Word and Holy Spirit;
fill with your grace all who partake
of the Body and Blood of our Lord Jesus Christ;
make us one Body that he may dwell in us and we in him.
And grant that with boldness
we may confess your Name in constancy of faith,
and at the last Day enter with all your Saints
into the joy of your eternal kingdom:

Through Jesus Christ our Lord,
by whom, and with whom, and in whom,
in the unity of the Holy Spirit
all honor and glory is yours,
O Father Almighty,
now and for ever.

Amen.

As our Savior Christ has taught us, we now pray,

Sursum Corda

[114]

The Lord be with you.   And also with you.
The Lord be with you.   And also with you.

Lift up your hearts.   We lift them up   to the Lord.
Lift up your hearts.   We lift them up un-to the Lord.

Let us give thanks to the Lord our God.
Let us give thanks unto our Lord God.

It is right to give him thanks and praise.
It is meet and right   so   to   do.

Sursum Corda

The Lord be   with you.   And al - so   with you.

Lift   up   your   hearts.   We lift   them up to   the Lord.

Let us give   thanks to the Lord our God.

It is right   to give him thanks and praise.

Prefaces Noted for Chant

It is very meet, right, and our boun-den du - ty, that we

should at all times, and in all places, give thanks un - to thee,

O Lord, Ho-ly Fa-ther, Al-migh-ty, Ev - er - last - ing God:

ADVENT

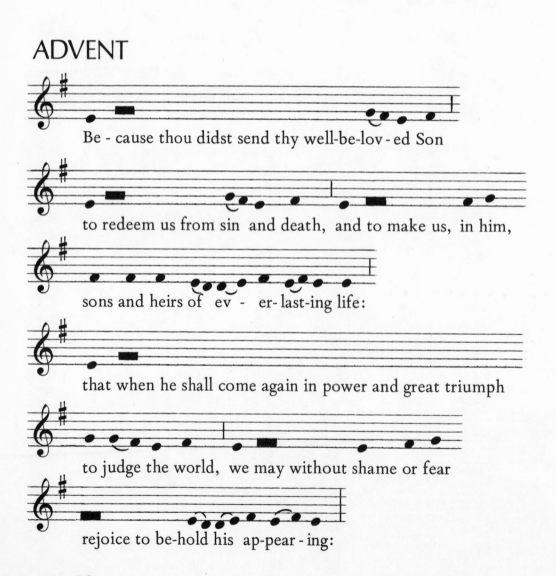

Be - cause thou didst send thy well-be-lov - ed Son

to redeem us from sin and death, and to make us, in him,

sons and heirs of ev - er - last-ing life:

that when he shall come again in power and great triumph

to judge the world, we may without shame or fear

rejoice to be-hold his ap-pear - ing:

CHRISTMAS

Be - cause thou didst give Jesus Christ, thine only Son,

to be born for us; who, by the mighty power of

the Ho-ly Spir - it, was made per-fect Man

of the flesh of the Virgin Ma - ry his moth-er;

that we, being delivered from the bon-dage of sin,

might receive power to be - come the sons of God:

* * * * * * * * * * * *

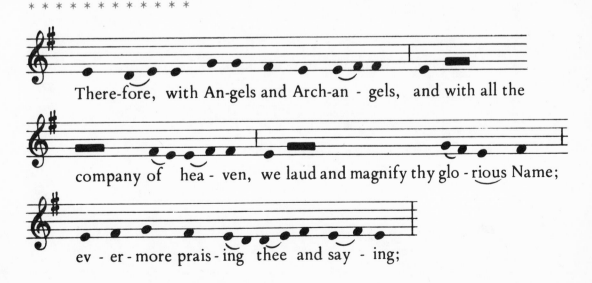

There-fore, with An-gels and Arch-an - gels, and with all the

company of hea - ven, we laud and magnify thy glo - rious Name;

ev - er -more prais-ing thee and say - ing;

It is very meet, right, and our boun-den du - ty, that we

should at all times, and in all places, give thanks un - to thee,

O Lord, Ho-ly Fa-ther, Al-migh-ty, Ev - er - last - ing God:

EPIPHANY

Through Je - sus Christ our Lord; who, in the substance

of our human nature, manifested his glo - ry:

that he might bring us out of dark - ness

in - to his own mar - velous light:

INCARNATION

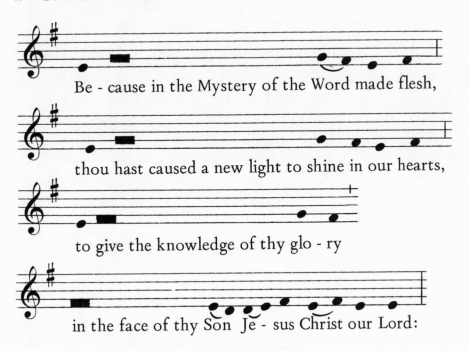

Be - cause in the Mystery of the Word made flesh,

thou hast caused a new light to shine in our hearts,

to give the knowledge of thy glo - ry

in the face of thy Son Je - sus Christ our Lord:

* * * * * * * * * * *

There-fore, with An-gels and Arch-an - gels, and with all the

company of hea - ven, we laud and magnify thy glo - rious Name;

ev - er - more prais - ing thee and say - ing;

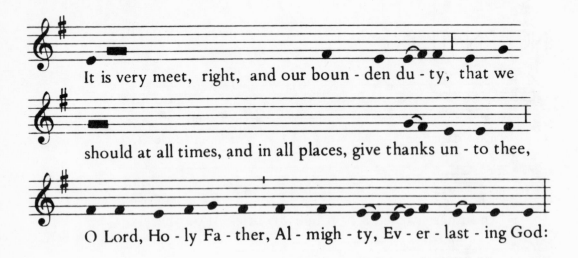

It is very meet, right, and our boun - den du - ty, that we

should at all times, and in all places, give thanks un - to thee,

O Lord, Ho - ly Fa - ther, Al - migh - ty, Ev - er - last - ing God:

LENT

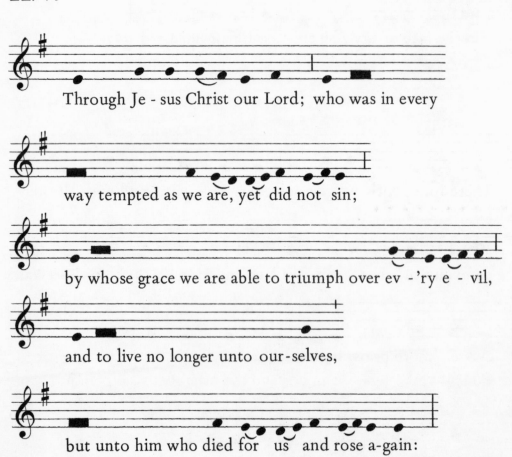

Through Je - sus Christ our Lord; who was in every

way tempted as we are, yet did not sin;

by whose grace we are able to triumph over ev -'ry e - vil,

and to live no longer unto our-selves,

but unto him who died for us and rose a-gain:

HOLY WEEK

Through Je - sus Christ our Lord;

who for our sins was lifted up up - on the Cross,

that he might draw all men to him - self;

who by his suf - f'ring and death be - came the way

of eternal sal - va - tion to all who o - bey him;

* * * * * * * * * * *

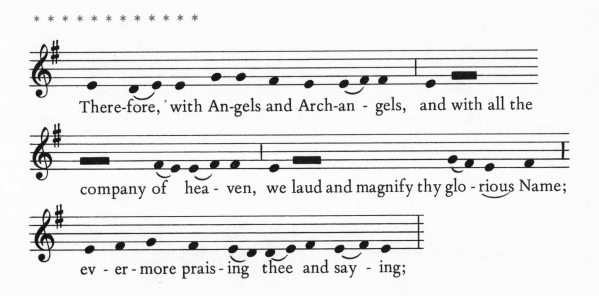

There-fore, with An-gels and Arch-an - gels, and with all the

company of hea - ven, we laud and magnify thy glo - rious Name;

ev - er - more prais-ing thee and say - ing;

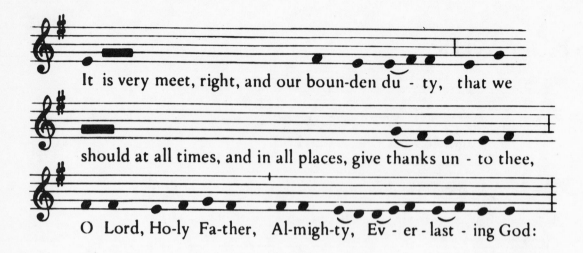

It is very meet, right, and our boun-den du - ty, that we
should at all times, and in all places, give thanks un - to thee,
O Lord, Ho-ly Fa-ther, Al-migh-ty, Ev - er - last - ing God:

EASTER

But chiefly are we bound to praise thee
for the glorious Re-sur-rec-tion of thy Son
Je - sus Christ our Lord, for he is the Pas - chal Lamb
who by his death hath o - ver - come death,
and by his rising to life a-gain
hath opened to us the way of ev - er - last-ing life:

ASCENSION

Through thy dearly beloved Son Jesus Christ our Lord;

who, after his glorious Resurrection,

openly appeared to all his A - post - les,

and in their sight was taken into hea - ven,

to pre - pare a place for us: that where he is,

there we might al - so be, and reign with him in glo - ry:

* * * * * * * * * * * *

There-fore, with An-gels and Arch-an - gels, and with all the

company of hea - ven, we laud and magnify thy glo - rious Name;

ev - er - more prais - ing thee and say - ing;

It is very meet, right, and our boun-den du - ty, that we

should at all times, and in all places, give thanks un - to thee,

O Lord, Ho-ly Fa-ther,   Al-migh-ty, Ev - er -last - ing God:

PENTECOST

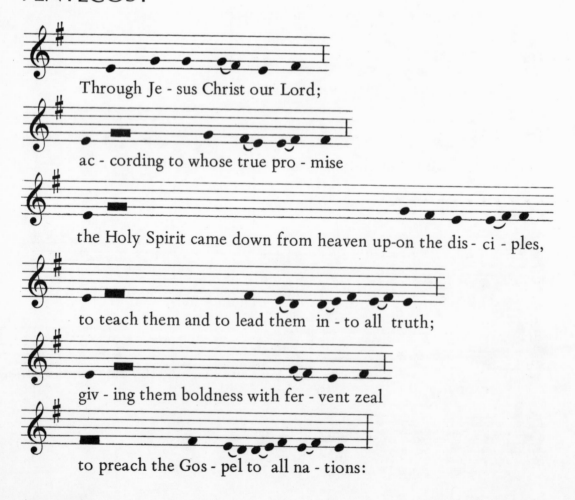

Through Je - sus Christ our Lord;

ac - cording to whose true pro - mise

the Holy Spirit came down from heaven up-on the dis - ci - ples,

to teach them and to lead them in - to all truth;

giv - ing them boldness with fer - vent zeal

to preach the Gos - pel to all na - tions:

TRINITY SUNDAY

Whom with thy co - eternal Son and Ho - ly Spir - it

we worship as one God, one Lord,

in Trinity of Per - sons and in U - ni - ty of Be - ing;

and we celebrate the one and e - qual glo - ry

of thee, O Father, and of the Son,

and of the Ho - ly Spir - it:

* * * * * * * * * * * *

There - fore, with An - gels and Arch - an - gels, and with all the

company of hea - ven, we laud and magnify thy glo - rious Name;

ev - er - more prais - ing thee and say - ing;

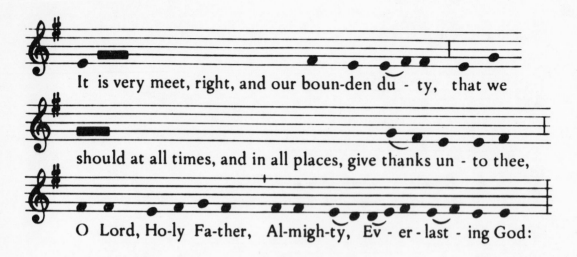

It is very meet, right, and our boun-den du - ty, that we

should at all times, and in all places, give thanks un - to thee,

O Lord, Ho-ly Fa-ther, Al-migh-ty, Ev - er - last - ing God:

THE LORD'S DAY I

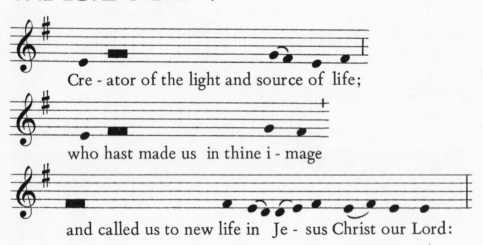

Cre - ator of the light and source of life;

who hast made us in thine i - mage

and called us to new life in Je - sus Christ our Lord:

THE LORD'S DAY II

Through Je - sus Christ our Lord,

who on this day overcame death and the grave,

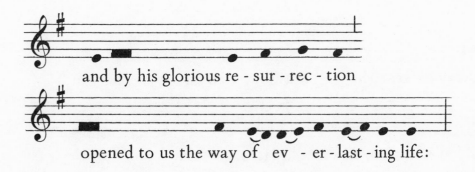

and by his glorious re - sur - rec - tion

opened to us the way of ev - er - last - ing life:

THE LORD'S DAY III

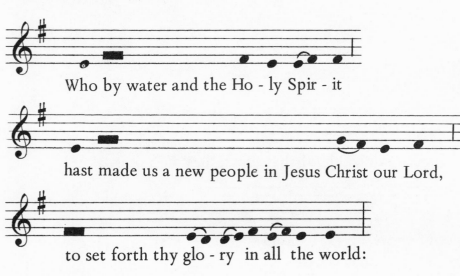

Who by water and the Ho - ly Spir - it

hast made us a new people in Jesus Christ our Lord,

to set forth thy glo - ry in all the world:

* * * * * * * * * * *

There-fore, with An-gels and Arch-an - gels, and with all the

company of hea - ven, we laud and magnify thy glo - rious Name;

ev - er - more prais - ing thee and say - ing;

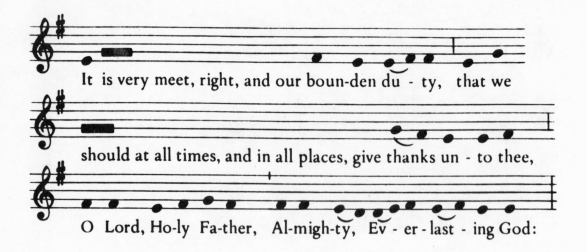

It is very meet, right, and our boun-den du - ty, that we

should at all times, and in all places, give thanks un - to thee,

O Lord, Ho-ly Fa-ther, Al-migh-ty, Ev - er - last - ing God:

ALL SAINTS

Who, in the multitude of thy saints, hast compassed

us about with so great a cloud of wit-nes-ses:

that we, rejoicing in their fel-low-ship,

may run with patience the race that is set be-fore us;

and, together with them, may receive

the crown of glo-ry that fa - deth not a-way:

APOSTLES

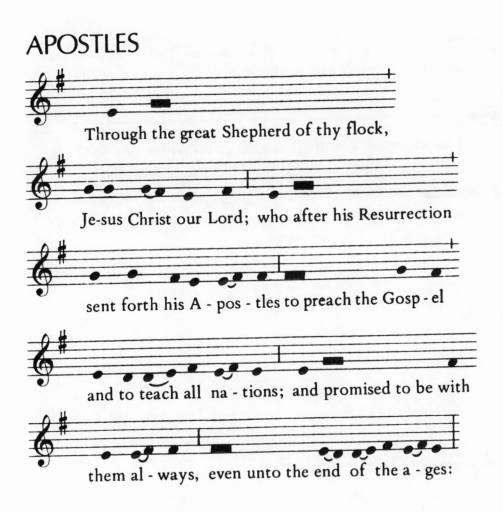

Through the great Shepherd of thy flock,

Je-sus Christ our Lord; who after his Resurrection

sent forth his A - pos - tles to preach the Gosp - el

and to teach all na - tions; and promised to be with

them al - ways, even unto the end of the a - ges:

* * * * * * * * * * * *

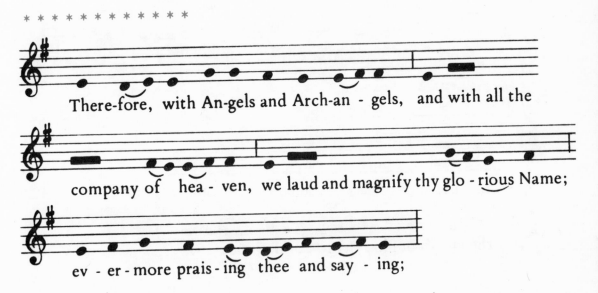

There-fore, with An-gels and Arch-an - gels, and with all the

company of hea - ven, we laud and magnify thy glo - rious Name;

ev - er - more prais-ing thee and say - ing;

It is very meet, right, and our boun-den du - ty, that we

should at all times, and in all places, give thanks un - to thee,

O Lord, Ho-ly Fa-ther, Al-migh-ty, Ev - er - last - ing God:

BAPTISM

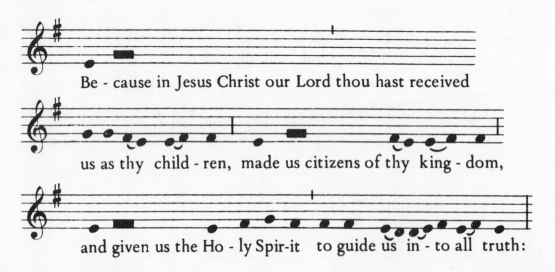

Be - cause in Jesus Christ our Lord thou hast received

us as thy child - ren, made us citizens of thy king - dom,

and given us the Ho - ly Spir-it to guide us in - to all truth:

MARRIAGE

Be - cause thou hast ordained the solemn covenant

of love between hus - band and wife

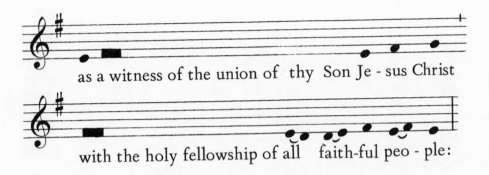

as a witness of the union of thy Son Je - sus Christ

with the holy fellowship of all faith-ful peo - ple:

COMMEMORATION OF THE DEAD

Through Je - sus Christ our Lord; who brought to light

the living hope of a blessed re - sur - rec - tion:

that in our grief we may rejoice in full as - sur - ance

of our change into the like-ness of his glo - ry:

* * * * * * * * * * * * *

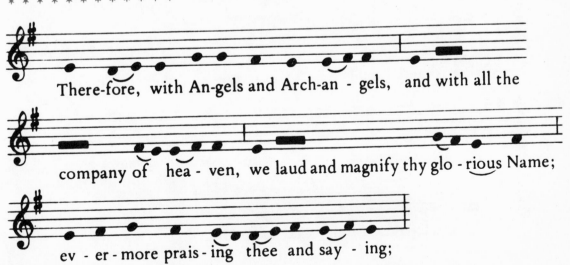

There-fore, with An-gels and Arch-an - gels, and with all the

company of hea - ven, we laud and magnify thy glo - rious Name;

ev - er-more prais-ing thee and say - ing;

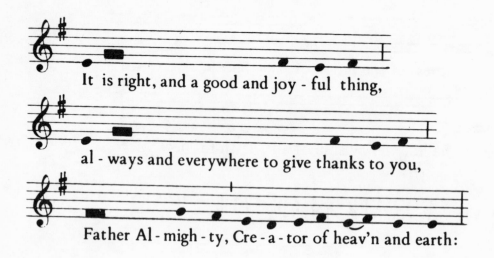

It is right, and a good and joy - ful thing,

al - ways and everywhere to give thanks to you,

Father Al - migh - ty, Cre - a - tor of heav'n and earth:

ADVENT

Be - cause you sent your well - beloved Son

to redeem us from sin and death, and to make us, in him,

sons and heirs of ev - er - last - ing life:

that when he shall come again in power and great triumph

to judge the world, we may without shame or fear

re - joice to be- hold his ap - pear - ing:

CHRISTMAS

Be - cause you gave Jesus Christ, your only Son,

to be born for us; who, by the mighty power of

the Ho - ly Spir - it, was made per - fect Man

of the flesh of the Vir - gin Ma - ry his moth - er:

that we, being delivered from the bon - dage of sin,

might receive power to be- come the sons of God:

* * * * * * * * * * * * *

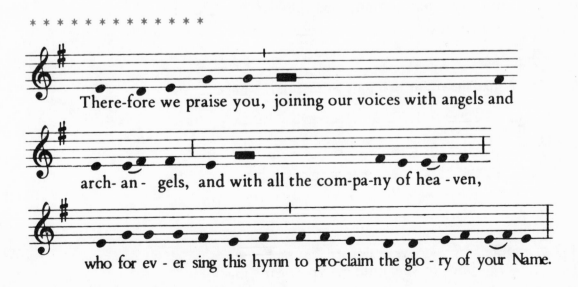

There-fore we praise you, joining our voices with angels and

arch- an - gels, and with all the com-pa-ny of hea -ven,

who for ev - er sing this hymn to pro-claim the glo - ry of your Name.

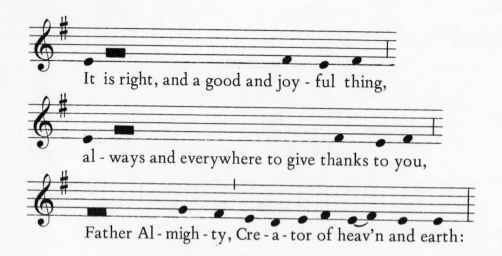

It is right, and a good and joy - ful thing,

al - ways and everywhere to give thanks to you,

Father Al - migh - ty, Cre - a - tor of heav'n and earth:

EPIPHANY

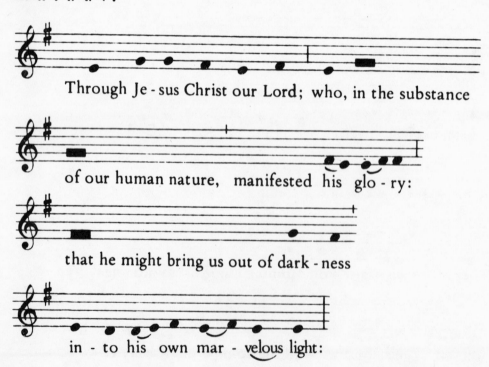

Through Je - sus Christ our Lord; who, in the substance

of our human nature, manifested his glo - ry:

that he might bring us out of dark - ness

in - to his own mar - velous light:

INCARNATION

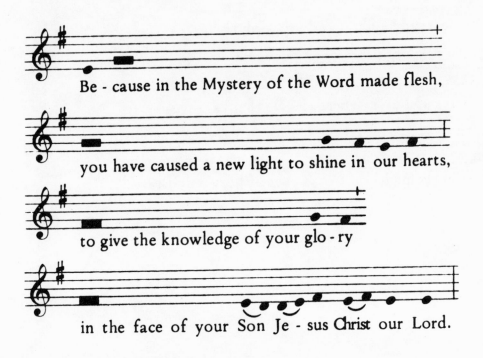

Be - cause in the Mystery of the Word made flesh,

you have caused a new light to shine in our hearts,

to give the knowledge of your glo - ry

in the face of your Son Je - sus Christ our Lord.

* * * * * * * * * * * * *

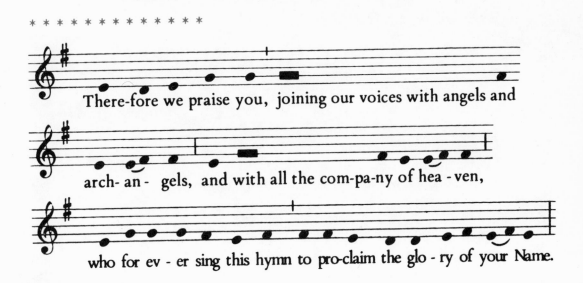

There-fore we praise you, joining our voices with angels and

arch- an - gels, and with all the com-pa-ny of hea - ven,

who for ev - er sing this hymn to pro-claim the glo - ry of your Name.

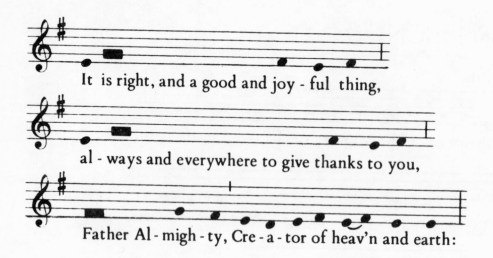

It is right, and a good and joy - ful thing,

al - ways and everywhere to give thanks to you,

Father Al - migh - ty, Cre - a - tor of heav'n and earth:

LENT

Through Je - sus Christ our Lord; who was in every

way tempted as we are, yet did not sin;

by whose grace we are able to triumph over ev - 'ry e - vil,

and to live no longer unto our - selves,

but unto him who died for us and rose a - gain:

HOLY WEEK

Through Je - sus Christ our Lord;

who for our sins was lifted up up - on the Cross,

that he might draw all men to him - self;

who by his suf - f'ring and death be - came the way

of eternal sal - va - tion to all who o - bey him:

* * * * * * * * * * * *

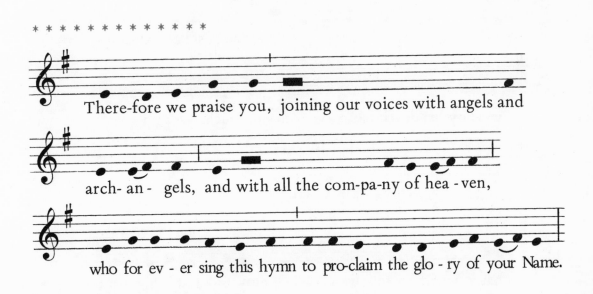

There-fore we praise you, joining our voices with angels and

arch- an - gels, and with all the com-pa-ny of hea -ven,

who for ev - er sing this hymn to pro-claim the glo - ry of your Name.

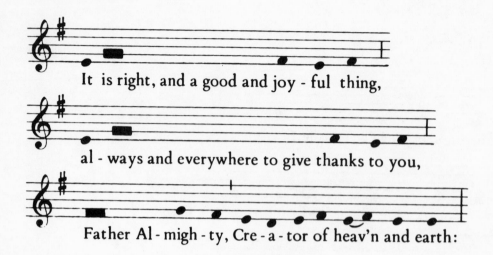

It is right, and a good and joy - ful thing,

al - ways and everywhere to give thanks to you,

Father Al - migh - ty, Cre - a - tor of heav'n and earth:

EASTER

But chiefly are we bound to praise you

for the glorious Re - sur - rec - tion of your Son

Je - sus Christ our Lord,   for he is the Paschal Lamb

who by his death has o - ver - come death,

and by his rising to life a - gain

has opened to us the way of ev - er - last - ing life:

ASCENSION

Through your dearly beloved Son Jesus Christ our Lord;

who, after his glorious Resurrection,

openly appeared to all his A - post - les,

and in their sight was taken into hea - ven,

to pre - pare a place for us: that where he is,

there we might al - so be, and reign with him in glo - ry:

* * * * * * * * * * * *

There-fore we praise you, joining our voices with angels and

arch- an - gels, and with all the com-pa-ny of hea - ven,

who for ev - er sing this hymn to pro-claim the glo - ry of your Name.

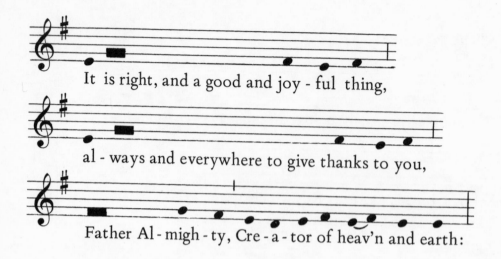

It is right, and a good and joy - ful thing,

al - ways and everywhere to give thanks to you,

Father Al - migh - ty, Cre - a - tor of heav'n and earth:

PENTECOST

Through Je - sus Christ our Lord;

ac - cording to whose true pro - mise the Holy Spirit

came down from heaven up - on the dis - ci - ples,

to teach them and to lead them in - to all truth;

giv - ing them boldness with fer - vent zeal

to preach the Gos - pel to all na - tions:

TRINITY SUNDAY

Whom with your co - eternal Son and Ho - ly Spir - it

we worship as one God, one Lord,

in Trinity of Per - sons and in U - ni - ty of Be - ing;

and we celebrate the one and e - qual glo - ry,

O Father, of you, and of the Son,

and of the Ho - ly Spir - it:

* * * * * * * * * * * * *

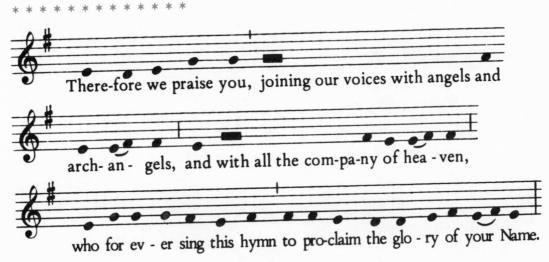

There-fore we praise you, joining our voices with angels and

arch- an - gels, and with all the com-pa-ny of hea - ven,

who for ev - er sing this hymn to pro-claim the glo - ry of your Name.

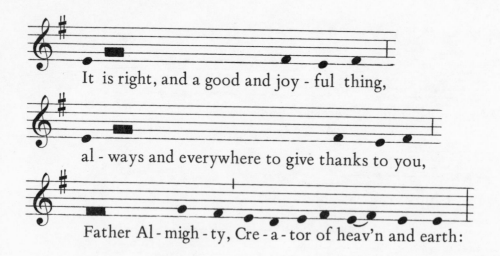

It is right, and a good and joy-ful thing,

al-ways and everywhere to give thanks to you,

Father Al-migh-ty, Cre-a-tor of heav'n and earth:

THE LORD'S DAY I

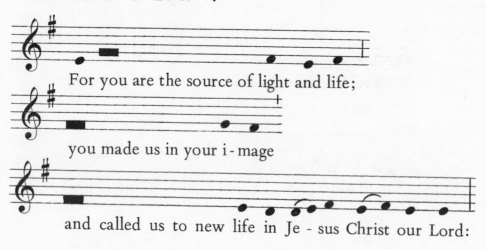

For you are the source of light and life;

you made us in your i-mage

and called us to new life in Je-sus Christ our Lord:

THE LORD'S DAY II

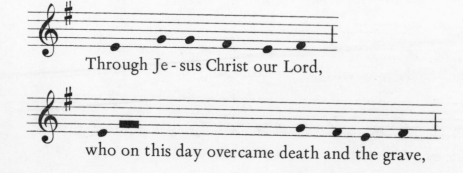

Through Je-sus Christ our Lord,

who on this day overcame death and the grave,

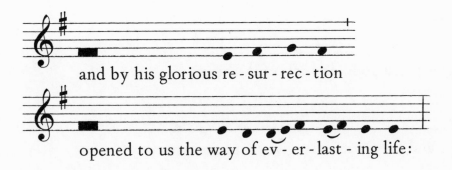

and by his glorious re - sur - rec - tion

opened to us the way of ev - er - last - ing life:

THE LORD'S DAY III

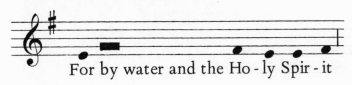

For by water and the Ho - ly Spir - it

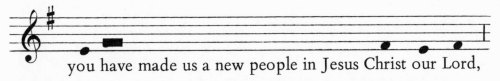

you have made us a new people in Jesus Christ our Lord,

to set forth your glo - ry in all the world:

* * * * * * * * * * * * *

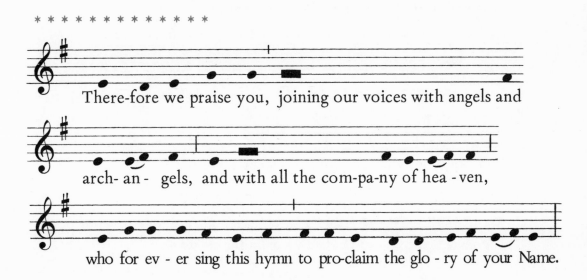

There-fore we praise you, joining our voices with angels and

arch- an - gels, and with all the com-pa-ny of hea - ven,

who for ev - er sing this hymn to pro-claim the glo - ry of your Name.

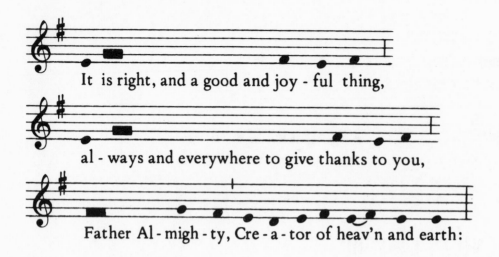

It is right, and a good and joy - ful thing,

al - ways and everywhere to give thanks to you,

Father Al - migh - ty, Cre - a - tor of heav'n and earth:

ALL SAINTS

For in the multitude of your saints, you have compassed

us about with so great a cloud of wit - nes - ses:

that we, rejoicing in their fel - low - ship,

may run with patience the race that is set be - fore us;

and, together with them, may receive

the crown of glo - ry that nev - er fades a - way:

APOSTLES

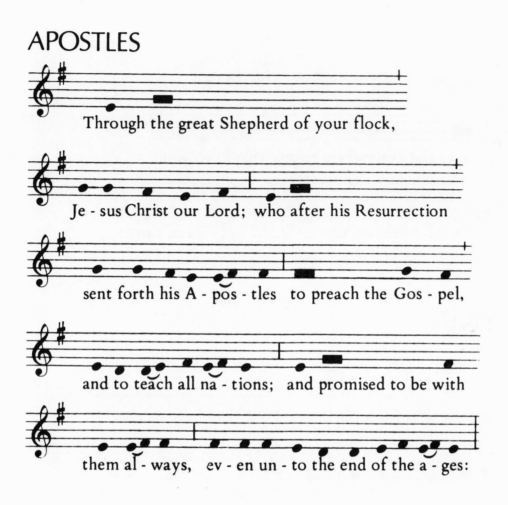

Through the great Shepherd of your flock,

Je - sus Christ our Lord; who after his Resurrection

sent forth his A - pos - tles to preach the Gos - pel,

and to teach all na - tions; and promised to be with

them al - ways, ev - en un - to the end of the a - ges:

* * * * * * * * * * * *

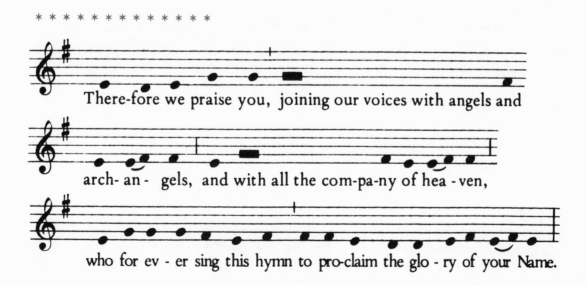

There-fore we praise you, joining our voices with angels and

arch- an - gels, and with all the com-pa-ny of hea - ven,

who for ev - er sing this hymn to pro-claim the glo - ry of your Name.

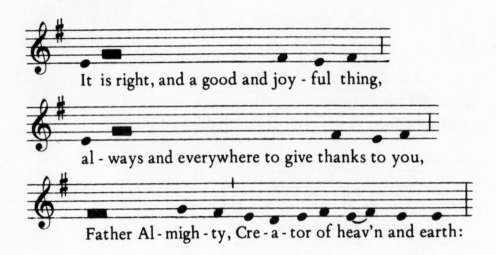

It is right, and a good and joy - ful thing,

al - ways and everywhere to give thanks to you,

Father Al - migh - ty, Cre - a - tor of heav'n and earth:

BAPTISM

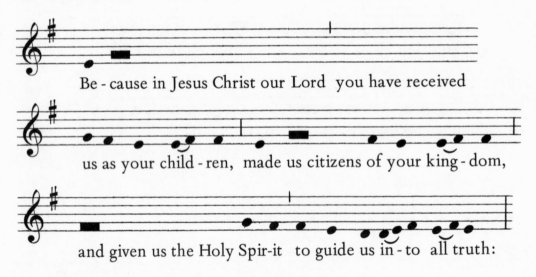

Be - cause in Jesus Christ our Lord you have received

us as your child - ren, made us citizens of your king - dom,

and given us the Holy Spir - it to guide us in - to all truth:

MARRIAGE

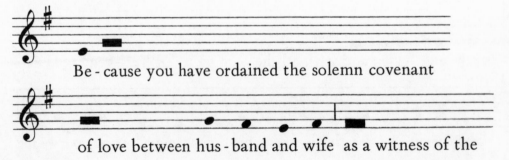

Be - cause you have ordained the solemn covenant

of love between hus - band and wife as a witness of the

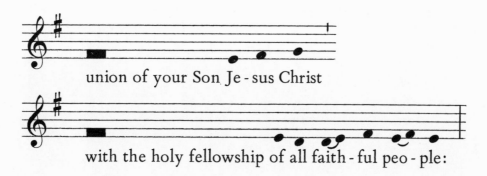

union of your Son Je-sus Christ

with the holy fellowship of all faith-ful peo-ple:

COMMEMORATION OF THE DEAD

Through Je-sus Christ our Lord; who brought to light

the living hope of a blessed re-sur-rec-tion:

that in our grief we may rejoice in full as-sur-ance

of our change into the like-ness of his glo-ry:

* * * * * * * * * * * * *

There-fore we praise you, joining our voices with angels and

arch-an- gels, and with all the com-pa-ny of hea-ven,

who for ev - er sing this hymn to pro-claim the glo-ry of your Name.

An Order For Celebrating The Holy Eucharist

which may be used on occasions other than the principal service on sundays and other feasts of our lord

[80] ORDER OF THE CELEBRATION

This order requires for its effective use careful preparation by all the worshippers so that all may understand what takes place and their own part in the celebration.

The use of silence, movement, and music will depend on the nature of the particular occasion.

THE PEOPLE AND PRIEST

gather in the lord's name

proclaim and respond to the word of god

the proclamation and response may include, in addition to a reading from the gospel, other readings, song, talk, dance, instrumental music, other art forms, silence.

pray for the world and the church

exchange the peace [81]

prepare the table

some of those present prepare the table; the bread, the cup of wine, and other offerings, are placed upon it.

make eucharist

the great thanksgiving is said by the priest in the name of the gathering, using one of the eucharistic prayers provided. In the course of the prayer, he takes the bread and cup into his hands, or places his hand upon them.

the people respond—amen!

break the bread

eat and drink together

the body and blood of the lord are shared in a reverent manner; after all have received, any of the sacrament that remains is then consumed.

When a common meal or agapé accompanies the celebration, it follows here.

[82] Eucharistic Prayers

In making Eucharist, the Priest uses one of the Eucharistic Prayers from the First or Second Service, or one of the following.

A

After a suitable invitation by the Priest, and a response by the People, the Priest gives thanks as follows:

We give thanks to you, O God our Creator;
You are worthy of praise from every creature you have made.
For in these last days you have sent your only Son
to be the Savior and Redeemer of the world.
In him, you have forgiven our sins,
and made us worthy to stand before you.
In him, you have brought us out of darkness into light
out of error into truth,
out of death into life.

On the night he was handed over to suffering and death,
our Lord Jesus Christ took bread;
and when he had given thanks to you,
he broke it, and gave it to his disciples,
and said, "Take this and eat it:
This is my Body, which is given for you.
Do this for the remembrance of me."

After supper he took the cup of wine,
and when he had given thanks, he gave it to them,
and said, "Drink this, all of you:
This is my Blood of the new Covenant,
which is shed for you and for many
for the forgiveness of sins.
Whenever you drink it, do this for the remembrance of me."

Remembering his death and resurrection,
we offer in thanksgiving this Bread and this Cup.
And we pray you to send your Holy Spirit
upon this Offering and upon your People,
to change us, and to make us one in your kingdom.
To you be praise and honor and worship
through your Son Jesus Christ
with the Holy Spirit
for ever and ever.

Amen.

B

After a suitable invitation by the Priest, and a response by the People, the Priest gives thanks as follows:

We give you thanks, O Father,
for the goodness and love
which you have made known to us in creation,
in the calling of Israel,
in the words of the prophets,
and, above all, in Jesus your Son:

Who, on the night before he died for us,
took bread and gave thanks;
he broke it and gave it to his disciples, and said:
"This is my body which is for you:
do this for my memorial."
In the same way,
he took the cup after supper and said:
"This cup is the new Covenant in my Blood.
Whenever you drink it,
do this for my memorial."

[84] Remembering now his suffering and death,
and celebrating his resurrection,
and looking for his coming again
to fulfill all things according to your will,
we ask you, Father,
through the power of the Holy Spirit,
to accept and bless these Gifts.
Make us one with your Son in his sacrifice,
that his life may be renewed in us.

And therefore, Father, through Jesus your Son,
in whom we have been accepted and made your children,
by your life-giving Spirit
we offer our grateful praise and say:

People and Priest

Our Father . . .

C

In the following Prayer, the italicized lines are spoken by the People.

The Lord be with you.
And also with you.

Lift up your hearts.
We lift them up to the Lord.

Let us give thanks to the Lord our God.
Let us praise him for his goodness now and for ever.

God of all power, Ruler of the Universe,
you are worthy of glory and praise.
Glory to you for ever and ever.

At your command all things came to be,
the vast expanse of interstellar space,

galaxies, suns, the planets in their courses, [85]
and this fragile earth, our island home:
By your will they were created and have their being.

From the primal elements you brought forth the race of
    man,
and blessed us with memory, reason, and skill;
you made us the rulers of creation.
But we turned against you, and betrayed your trust;
and we turned against one another.
Have mercy, Lord, for we are sinners in your sight.

Again and again, you called us to return.
Through prophets and sages you revealed your righteous
    Law;
and in the fullness of time, you sent your only Son,
born of a woman, to fulfill your Law,
to open for us the way of freedom and peace.
By his blood, he reconciled us.
By his wounds, we are healed.

[And, therefore, we praise you,
  joining with the heavenly chorus,
  with prophets, apostles, and martyrs,
  and with men of every generation
    who have looked to you in hope:
to proclaim with them your glory,
in their unending hymn:

Priest and People

Holy, holy, holy Lord, God of power and might,
heaven and earth are full of your glory.
    Hosanna in the highest.
Blessed is he who comes in the name of the Lord.
    Hosanna in the highest.]

[86]   The Priest continues

And so, Father, we who have been redeemed by him,
and made a new people by water and the Spirit,
now bring before you these gifts.
Sanctify them by your Holy Spirit
to be for us the Body and Blood
of Jesus Christ our Lord.

On the night he was betrayed,
he took bread, said the blessing,
broke the bread, and gave it to his friends,
and said, "Take this and eat it.
This is my Body, which is given for you.
Do this for the remembrance of me."

In the same way, after supper, he took the cup,
and said "Drink of this, all of you.
This is my Blood of the new Covenant,
which is poured out for you and for all mankind
for the forgiveness of sins.
Whenever you drink it, do this for the remembrance of me."

Priest and People

When we eat this Bread
and drink this Cup,
we show forth your death, Lord Christ,
until you come in glory.

Priest

Lord God of our Fathers,
God of Abraham, Isaac, and Jacob,
God and Father of our Lord Jesus Christ:
open our eyes to see your hand at work in the world
    about us.

Deliver us from the presumption of coming to this Table [87]
for solace only, and not for strength;
for pardon only, and not for renewal.
Let the grace of this Holy Communion
make us one body, one spirit in Christ,
that we may worthily serve the world in his name.
Risen Lord, be known to us in the breaking of the Bread.

Accept these prayers and praises, Father,
through Jesus Christ, our great High Priest,
to whom with you and the Holy Spirit,
your Church gives honor, glory, and worship,
from generation to generation.

Amen.

D

Priest   The grace of our Lord Jesus Christ and the love
of God and the fellowship of the Holy Spirit be
with you all.

or   The Lord be with you.

People   And also with you.

Priest   Lift up your hearts.
People   We lift them up to the Lord.

Priest   Let us give thanks to the Lord our God.
People   It is right to give him thanks and praise.

The Priest begins the Prayer with these or similar words:

Father, we thank you and we praise you . . .

He gives thanks for God's work in Creation
and his revelation of himself to men.

[88]   He may recall before God the particular occasion
being celebrated.

He may incorporate or adapt the Proper Preface of the day.

[If the Sanctus is to be included he leads into it with these or
similar words:

> And so we join the saints and angels
> in proclaiming your glory as we sing (say),
>
> Holy, holy, holy Lord . . .]

Here he praises God for the salvation of the world through
Jesus Christ our Lord.

He then continues with these words

And so, Father, we bring you these gifts.
Sanctify them by your Holy Spirit
to be for your People the Body and Blood
of Jesus Christ our Lord.

On the night he was betrayed,
he took bread, said the blessing,
broke the bread, and gave it to his friends,
and said, "Take this and eat it.
This is my Body, which is given for you.
Do this for the remembrance of me."

In the same way, after the supper, he took the cup,
and said "Drink of this, all of you.
This is my Blood of the new Covenant,
which is poured out for you and for all men
for the forgiveness of sins.
Whenever you drink it, do this for the remembrance of me."

Father, we now celebrate the memorial of your Son. [89]
By means of this holy Bread and Cup,
we show forth the sacrifice of his death
and proclaim his resurrection
until he comes again.

Gather us by this Holy Communion
into one Body in your Son Jesus Christ.
Make us a living sacrifice of praise.

By him, and with him, and in him,
in the unity of the Holy Spirit
all honor and glory is yours,
Almighty Father,
now and for ever.

Amen.

Forms of Intercession

FORMS OF INTERCESSION [93]

Prayer is offered with intercession for

The Universal Church and all its members

The Nation and all in authority

The welfare of the world

The concerns of the local community

Those who suffer and those in any trouble

The departed (with commemoration of a saint when appropriate)

If a confession of sin is not said at the service, a form of Intercession containing a penitential petition should be chosen. [For example: I, V, or VII.]

The Priest may introduce the Prayers with a sentence of invitation related to the Season or the Proper of the Day.

When a briefer form of Prayer is desired, some or all of the petitions marked with an asterisk may be omitted.

I

Deacon or other leader

With all our heart and with all our mind, let us pray to the Lord, saying, "Lord, have mercy".

* For the peace from above, for the loving kindness of God, and for the salvation of our souls,
let us pray to the Lord.

Lord, have mercy.

For the peace of the world, for the welfare of the holy Church of God, and for the unity of all mankind,
let us pray to the Lord.

Lord, have mercy.

[94]   For our Bishop, and for all the clergy and people,
let us pray to the Lord.

Lord, have mercy.

For our President, for the leaders of the nations, and for
all in authority,
let us pray to the Lord.

Lord, have mercy.

For this city (*town, village,* . . .), for every city and community, and for those who live in them,
let us pray to the Lord.

Lord, have mercy.

* For seasonable weather, and for an abundance of the
fruits of the earth,
let us pray to the Lord.

Lord, have mercy.

* For the good earth which God has given us, and for the
wisdom and will to conserve it,
let us pray to the Lord.

Lord, have mercy.

* For those who travel on land, on water, in the air, or
through outer space,
let us pray to the Lord.

Lord, have mercy.

For the aged and infirm, for widows and orphans, and for
the sick and the suffering,
let us pray to the Lord.

Lord, have mercy.

For the poor and the oppressed, for prisoners and captives, [95]
and for all who remember and care for them,
let us pray to the Lord.

Lord, have mercy.

For all who have died in the hope of the resurrection, and
for all the departed,
let us pray to the Lord.

Lord, have mercy.

* For deliverance from all danger, violence, oppression,
and degradation,
let us pray to the Lord.

Lord, have mercy.

* For the absolution and remission of our sins and offenses,
let us pray to the Lord.

Lord, have mercy.

* That we may end our lives in faith and hope, without
suffering and without reproach,
let us pray to the Lord.

Lord, have mercy.

* Defend us, deliver us, and in *thy* compassion protect us,
O Lord, by *thy* grace.

Lord, have mercy.

In the Communion of Saints, let us commend ourselves,
and one another, and all our life, to Christ our God.

To thee, O Lord our God.

A brief silence is then observed.

[96]   The Priest concludes with the following or some other prayer:

Lord Jesus Christ: *who hast* given us grace at this time with one accord to make our common supplication; and *hast* promised that when two or three are agreed together in *thy* Name *thou wilt* grant their requests; Fulfill now, O Lord, our desires and petitions, as may be best for us; granting us in this world knowledge of *thy* truth, and in the world to come life everlasting; through *thy* mercy, O Christ, to whom with the Father and the Holy Spirit be honor and glory for ever and ever. *Amen.*

II

In the course of the silence after each bidding, the People offer their own prayers, either silently or aloud.

I ask your prayers for God's people throughout the world: for our Bishop(s) ____; for this gathering; and for all ministers and people.
Pray, brothers, for the Church.

Silence

I ask your prayers for peace among men; for goodwill among nations; and for the well-being of all people.
Pray, brothers, for justice and peace.

Silence

I ask your prayers for the poor, the sick, the hungry, the oppressed, and those in prison.
Pray, brothers, for those in any need or trouble.

Silence

I ask your prayers for all who seek God, or a deeper [97]
knowledge of him.
Pray, brothers, that they may find and be found of him.

Silence

I ask your prayers for the departed [especially _____].
Pray, brothers, for those who have died.

Silence

Members of the congregation may ask the prayers or the thanksgiving of those present.

* I ask your prayers for . . .

* I ask your thanksgiving for . . .
Give thanks, brothers, for God's great goodness.

Silence

Praise God for those in every generation in whom Christ
has been honored [especially _____ whom we remember
today]. And pray that we may have grace to glorify Christ
in our own day.

Silence

The Priest adds a concluding collect.

III
(Traditional Form)

After the Priest's invitation to prayer, the Leader and People pray responsively.

Father, we pray for thy holy Catholic Church:
That we all may be one.

Grant that every member of the Church may truly and humbly serve thee:
That thy Name may be glorified by all people.

We pray for all Bishops, Priests and Deacons:
That they may be faithful stewards of thy holy mysteries.

We pray for all who govern and hold authority in the nations of the world:
That there may be peace and justice among men.

May we seek to do thy will in all that we undertake:
That we may be blest in all our works.

Have compassion on those who suffer from any grief or trouble:
That they may be delivered from their distress.

Grant rest eternal to the departed:
Let light perpetual shine upon them.

We praise thee for all thy saints who have entered into joy:
May we also come to share in thy heavenly kingdom.

Let us pray in silence for our own needs and those of others.

Silence

The Priest concludes with this or some other collect:

Almighty God, the fountain of all wisdom, who knowest [99] our necessities before we ask, and our ignorance in asking: We beseech thee to have compassion upon our infirmities; and those things which for our unworthiness we dare not, and for our blindness cannot ask, mercifully give us for the sake of thy Son Jesus Christ our Lord. *Amen.*

III

(Contemporary Form)

After the Priest's invitation to prayer, the Leader and People pray responsively.

Father, we pray for your holy Catholic Church:
That we all may be one.

Grant that every member of the Church may truly and humbly serve you:
That your Name may be glorified by all people.

We pray for all Bishops, Priests and Deacons:
That they may be faithful ministers of your Word and Sacraments.

We pray for all who govern and hold authority in the nations of the world:
That there may be peace and justice among men.

Give us courage to do your will in all that we undertake:
That we may be blest in all our works.

Have compassion on those who suffer from any grief or trouble:
That they may be delivered from their distress.

[100] Give to the departed eternal rest:
Let your light shine upon them for ever.

We praise you for all your saints who have entered into joy:
May we also come to share in your heavenly kingdom.

Let us pray in silence for our own needs and those of others.

Silence

The Priest concludes with this or some other collect:

Almighty God, to whom our needs are known before we ask, help us to ask only what accords with your will; and those good things which we dare not, or in our blindness cannot ask, grant us for the sake of your Son, Jesus Christ our Lord. *Amen.*

IV

The Leader may expand any paragraph with specific petitions. A short period of silence follows each paragraph. The periods of silence may be concluded as follows:

Lord, in your mercy
Hear our prayer.

Let us pray for the whole Church of God in Christ Jesus, and for all men according to their needs.

Silence

Grant, Almighty God, that we who confess your Name may be united in your truth, live together in your love, and show forth your glory in the world.

Silence

Direct this and every nation into the ways of justice and ~~[101]~~ peace, that we may honor all men, and seek the common good.

> Silence

Save and comfort those who suffer, that they may hold to you through good and ill, and trust in your unfailing love.

> Silence

Remember, Lord, those who have died in the peace of Christ, and those whose faith is known to you alone, and deal with us and them according to your great mercy.

> Silence

Grant these our prayers, O merciful Father, for the sake of your Son, our Savior Jesus Christ. *Amen.*

V

> Deacon or other leader

In peace, let us pray to the Lord, saying

> "Lord, have mercy"
> or   "Kyrie eleison".

For the peace of the world, that a spirit of respect and forbearance may grow among nations and peoples, we pray to you, O Lord.

> Here and after every petition the People respond:

> *Kyrie eleison.*
> or   *Lord, have mercy.*

For the holy Church of God, that it may be filled with truth and love, and be found without fault at the Day of your Coming, we pray to you, O Lord.

[102] For *N.* our Presiding Bishop, for *N. (N.)* our own Bishop(s), for all Bishops and other Ministers, and for all the holy People of God,
we pray to you, O Lord.

* For all who fear God and believe in his Christ, that our divisions may cease and all may be one as you, Lord, and the Father are one,
we pray to you, O Lord.

* For the mission of the Church, that in faithful witness it may preach the Gospel to the ends of the earth,
we pray to you, O Lord.

* For those who do not yet believe, and for those who have lost their faith, that they may receive the light of the Gospel,
we pray to you, O Lord.

For those in positions of public trust, [especially _____], that they may serve justice, and promote the dignity and freedom of all men,
we pray to you, O Lord.

* For a blessing upon the labors of men, and for the right use of the riches of creation, that mankind may be freed from famine and disaster,
we pray to you, O Lord.

For the poor, the persecuted, the sick, and all who suffer; for refugees, prisoners, and all who are in danger: that they may be relieved and protected,
we pray to you, O Lord.

For this Congregation; for those who are present, and for [103] those who are absent, that we may be delivered from hardness of heart, and show forth your glory in all that we do,
we pray to you, O Lord.

* For our enemies and those who wish us harm; and for all whom we have injured or offended,
  we pray to you, O Lord.

* For ourselves; for the forgiveness of our sins, and for the grace of the Holy Spirit to amend our lives,
  we pray to you, O Lord,

For all who have commended themselves to our prayers: for our families, friends, and neighbors; that being freed from anxiety, they may live in joy, peace, and health,
we pray to you, O Lord.

* For _____,
  we pray to you, O Lord.

For all who have died in the faith of Christ, that, with all the saints, they may have rest in that place where there is no pain or grief, but life eternal,
we pray to you, O Lord.

Rejoicing in the fellowship of [the ever-blessed Virgin Mary, (*blessed N.*) and] all the saints, let us commend ourselves, and one another, and all our life to Christ our God.

To you, O Lord our God.

Silence

[104]   The Priest says this doxology:

For yours is the Majesty, O Father, Son, and Holy Spirit;
yours is the kingdom and the power and the glory,
now and for ever. *Amen.*

or else he concludes with this or some other prayer:

O Lord our God, accept the fervent prayers of your people;
in the multitude of your mercies, look with compassion
upon us and all who turn to you for help: For you are
gracious, O lover of men; and to you we give glory, Father,
Son, and Holy Spirit, now and for ever. *Amen.*

VI

The specific petitions that are indented may be adapted by
addition or omission, as appropriate, at the discretion of the
Minister. The collects which follow each period of silent prayer
are customarily said by the Priest. Each collect is printed twice:
first in contemporary and then in traditional language.

Deacon or other leader

Let us pray for all men everywhere according to their
need, and for the people of God in every place.

Let us pray for the holy Catholic Church of Christ
throughout the world; especially,

    For its unity in witness and service
    For all Bishops and other Ministers
        and the people whom they serve
    For N., our Bishop, and all the people of this Diocese
    For all Christians in this community
    For those preparing to be baptized (particularly, . . .)

that God will confirm his church in faith, increase it in [105]
love, and preserve it in peace.

Silence

Almighty and everlasting God, by whose Spirit the whole company of your faithful people is governed and sanctified: Receive our prayers which we now offer before you for all members of your holy Church, that in their vocation and ministry they may truly and devoutly serve you, to the glory of your Name; through our Lord and Savior Jesus Christ. *Amen.*

Almighty and everlasting God, by whose Spirit the whole body of the Church is governed and sanctified: Receive our supplications and prayers, which we offer before thee for all members of thy holy Church, that every member of the same, in his vocation and ministry, may truly and godly serve thee; through our Lord and Savior Jesus Christ. *Amen.*

Let us pray for all nations and peoples of the earth, and for those in authority among them; especially,

> For *N.*, the President of the United States
> For the Congress and the Supreme Court
> For the Members and representatives of the United
>   Nations
> For all who serve the common good of men

that by God's help they may seek justice and truth, and live in peace and concord.

Silence

Almighty God, from whom all thoughts of truth and peace proceed: We pray you to kindle in the hearts of all men the true love of peace; and guide with your pure and

[106] peaceable wisdom those who take counsel for the nations of the earth, that in tranquillity your kingdom may go forward, until the earth is filled with the knowledge of your love; through Jesus Christ our Lord. *Amen.*

Almighty God, from whom all thoughts of truth and peace proceed: Kindle, we pray thee, in the hearts of all men the true love of peace; and guide with thy pure and peaceable wisdom those who take counsel for the nations of the earth; that in tranquillity thy kingdom may go forward, till the earth is filled with the knowledge of thy love; through Jesus Christ our Lord. *Amen.*

Let us pray for all who suffer, and are afflicted in body or in mind; especially,

> For the hungry and the homeless, the destitute and the oppressed
> For the sick, the wounded, and the crippled
> For those in loneliness, fear, and anguish
> For those who face temptation, doubt, and despair
> For prisoners and captives, and those in mortal danger
> For the sorrowful and bereaved

that God in his mercy will comfort and relieve them, and grant them the knowledge of his love, and stir up in us the will and patience to minister to their needs.

Silence

Gracious God, you see all the suffering, injustice, and misery which abound in this world. We implore you to look mercifully upon the poor, the oppressed, and all who are burdened with pain and sorrow. Fill our hearts with your compassion, and give us strength to serve them in their need, for the sake of him who suffered for us, our Savior Jesus Christ. *Amen.*

Gracious God, who seest all the suffering, injustice, and misery which abound in this world: We beseech thee to look mercifully upon the poor, the oppressed, and all who are burdened with pain and sorrow. Fill our hearts with thy compassion, and give us strength to serve them in their need, for the sake of him who suffered for us, our Savior Jesus Christ. *Amen.*

Let us pray for all who, whether in ignorance or in disbelief, have not received the gospel of Christ; especially,

> For those who have never heard the word of Christ
> For those who have lost their faith
> For those hardened by sin or indifference
> For the contemptuous and the scornful
> For those who are enemies of the Cross of Christ,
>   and persecutors of his disciples

that God will open their hearts to the truth, and lead them to faith and obedience.

Silence

Merciful God, who made all men and hate nothing that you have made; nor do you desire the death of a sinner, but rather that he should be converted and live: Have mercy upon all who know you not as you are revealed in the Gospel of your Son. Take from them all ignorance, hardness of heart, and contempt of your Word. Bring all men home, good Lord, to your fold, so that they may be one flock under the one shepherd, your Son Jesus Christ our Lord. *Amen.*

Merciful God, who hast made all men, and hatest nothing that thou hast made, nor desirest the death of a sinner, but rather that he should be converted and live: Have

[108] mercy upon all who know thee not as thou art revealed in the Gospel of thy Son. Take from them all ignorance, hardness of heart, and contempt of thy Word; and so bring them home, blessed Lord, to thy fold, that they may be made one flock under one shepherd, Jesus Christ our Lord. *Amen.*

Let us commit ourselves to our God, and pray for the grace of a holy life, that, with all who have departed this world and have died in the faith, we may be accounted worthy to enter into the fullness of the joy of our Lord, and receive the crown of life in the day of resurrection.

Silence

O God of unchangeable power and eternal light: Look favorably on your whole Church, that wonderful and sacred mystery. By the tranquil operation of your providence, carry out the work of man's salvation. Let the whole world see and know that things which were cast down are being raised up, and things which had grown old are being made new, and that all things are being renewed to the perfection of him through whom all things were made, your Son our Lord Jesus Christ, who lives and reigns with you, in the unity of the Holy Spirit, one God, for ever and ever. *Amen.*

O God of unchangeable power and eternal light: Look favorably upon thy whole Church, that wonderful and sacred mystery; and by the tranquil operation of thy providence, carry out the work of man's salvation. Let the whole world see and know that things which were cast down are being raised up, and things which had grown old are being made new, and that all things are

126

being renewed unto the perfection of him through whom [109] all things were made, thy Son our Lord Jesus Christ, who liveth and reigneth with thee in the unity of the Holy Spirit, one God, for ever and ever. *Amen.*

VII

The Leader and People pray responsively

In peace, we pray to you, Lord God:

For all people in their daily life and work;
For our families, friends, and neighbors, and for those who are alone.

For this community, the nation, and the world;
For all who work for justice, freedom, and peace.

For the just and proper use of your creation;
For the victims of hunger, fear, injustice and oppression.

For all who are in danger, sorrow, or any kind of trouble;
For those who minister to the sick, the friendless, and the needy.

For the peace and unity of the Church of God;
For all who proclaim the Gospel, and all who seek the Truth.

For Bishops and other Ministers, [especially for *N.* our Presiding Bishop, and *N.(N.)* our Bishop(s)];
For all who serve God in his Church.

For the special needs and concerns of this congregation.

Those present may add their own petitions.

[110]   Hear us, Lord;
           For your mercy is great.

We thank you, Lord, for all the blessings of this life.

The People may add their own thanksgivings

           We will exalt you, O God our King;
           And praise your Name for ever and ever.

We pray for all who have died, [especially _____], that they may have a place in your eternal kingdom.

           Lord, let your loving-kindness be upon them;
           Who put their trust in you.

* We pray to you also for the forgiveness of our sins.

Leader and People

           Have mercy upon us, most merciful Father:
           In your compassion forgive us our sins,
               known and unknown, things done and left undone:
           And so uphold us by your Spirit
           that we may live and serve you in newness of life,
               to the honor and glory of your Name.

The Priest concludes the prayers with a suitable collect.

Concerning the Collect at the Prayers [111]

When a Collect concludes the Intercession, a suitable one is selected, such as:

(a) a collect appropriate to the Season or occasion being celebrated;
(b) a collect expressive of some special need in the life of the local congregation;
(c) a collect for the mission of the Church;
(d) a general collect such as the following:

Lord, hear the prayers of your people; and what we have asked faithfully, grant that we may obtain effectually, to the glory of your Name; through Jesus Christ our Lord. *Amen.*

Heavenly Father, you have promised to hear what we ask in the Name of your Son: We pray you, accept and fulfill our petitions, not as we ask in our ignorance, nor as we deserve in our sinfulness, but as you know and love us in your Son, Jesus Christ our Lord. *Amen.*

Almighty and eternal God, ruler of all things in heaven and earth: Mercifully accept the prayers of your people, and strengthen us to do your will; through Jesus Christ our Lord. *Amen.*

Hasten, O Father, the coming of your Kingdom; and grant that we your servants, who now live by faith, may with joy behold your Son at his coming in glorious majesty; even Jesus Christ, our only Mediator and Advocate. *Amen.*

[112] Lord Jesus Christ, you said to your Apostles, "Peace I give to you; my own peace I leave with you": Regard not our sins, but the faith of your Church, and give to us the peace and unity of that heavenly City where, with the Father and the Holy Spirit, you live and reign now and for ever. *Amen.*

O God, you have brought us near to an innumerable company of angels, and to the spirits of just men made perfect: Grant us during our earthly pilgrimage to abide in their fellowship, and in our heavenly country to become partakers of their joy; through Jesus Christ our Lord. *Amen.*

God grant to the living—grace;
        to the departed—rest;
        to the church, the nation, and all mankind—
            peace and concord;
        and to us and all his servants—life everlasting. *Amen.*

[For additional Collects]

HOLY EUCHARIST

SUGGESTED OFFERTORY SENTENCES [112]

One of the following, or some other appropriate Sentence of Scripture, may be used in place of the Offertory Sentence provided in the text of the Service.

Walk in love, as Christ loved us and gave himself for us, an offering and sacrifice to God. (*Ephesians 5:2*)

I pray you brethren, by the mercies of God, to present yourselves as a living sacrifice, holy and acceptable to God, which is your spiritual worship. (*Romans 12:1*)

If you are offering your gift at the altar, and there remember that your brother has something against you, leave your gift there before the altar and go; first be reconciled to your brother, and then come and offer your gift. (*Matthew 5:23–24*) [113]

Thine, O Lord, is the greatness, and the power, and the glory, and the victory, and the majesty. For all that is in the heaven and in the earth is thine. Thine is the kingdom, O Lord, and thou art exalted as head above all.
(*1 Chronicles 29:11*)

Yours, O Lord, is the greatness, the power, the glory, the victory, and the majesty. For everything in the heaven and on earth is yours. Yours, O Lord, is the kingdom, and you are exalted as head over all. (*1 Chronicles 29:11*)

Worthy art thou, our Lord and God, to receive glory and honor and power; for thou hast created all things, and by thy will they exist and were created. (*Revelation 4:11*)

O Lord our God: you are worthy to receive glory and honor and power; because you have created all things; and by your will they were created and have their being. (*Revelation 4:11*)

or this Bidding:

Let us with gladness present the offerings and oblations of our life and labor unto the Lord.

At the Easter Vigil

The Lighting of the Paschal Candle takes place either before the singing of the Exsultet, or in the course of it (at the point indicated on page 140).

The Exsultet is properly sung by a deacon or priest. It may, however (if necessary), be sung by a lay cantor.

When a shorter form is desired, one or more of the bracketed sections may be omitted.

Exsultet

[521]

Re - joice now, hea - ven - ly hosts, and choirs of an - gels,

and let your trum - pets shout Sal - va - tion

for the vic - to - ry of our might - y King.

Re - joice and sing now, all the round earth,

bright with a glo - ri - ous splen - dor,

for dark - ness has been van - quished by our e - ter - nal King.

135

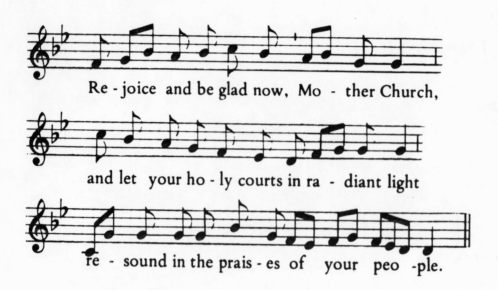

Re - joice and be glad now, Mo - ther Church,

and let your ho - ly courts in ra - diant light

re - sound in the prais - es of your peo -ple.

All you who stand near this mar - vel - ous, ho - ly flame,

pray with me to God the Al - might -y for grace

to sing the wor - thy praise of this great light;

through Je - sus Christ his Son our Lord,

who lives and reigns with him, in the u - ni - ty of the

Ho - ly Spir - it, one God, for ev - er and ev - er. A - men.

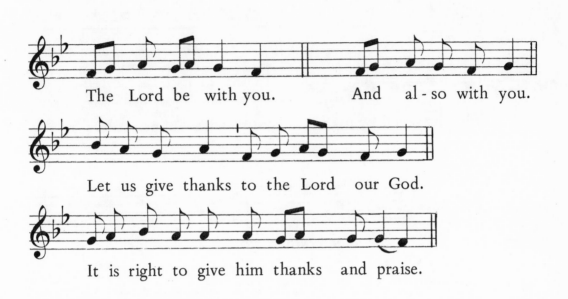

The Lord be with you.   And al - so with you.

Let us give thanks to the Lord   our God.

It is right to give him thanks   and praise.

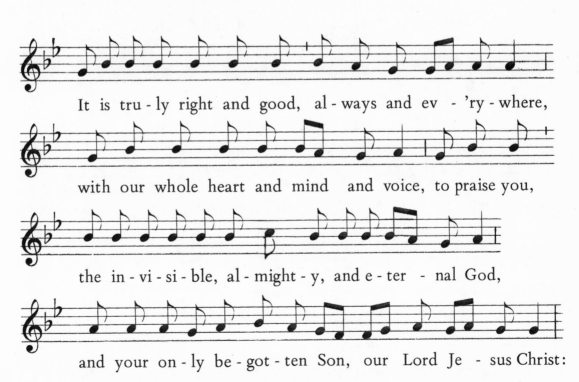

It is tru - ly right and good, al - ways and ev - 'ry - where,

with our whole heart and mind   and voice, to praise you,

the in - vi - si - ble, al - might - y, and e - ter - nal God,

and your on - ly be - got - ten Son, our Lord Je - sus Christ:

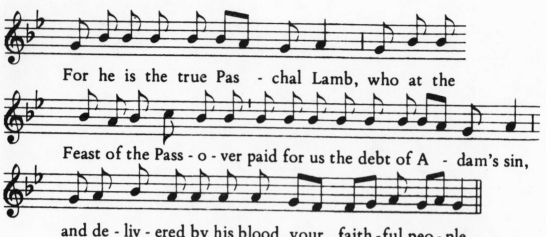

For he is the true Pas - chal Lamb, who at the

Feast of the Pass - o - ver paid for us the debt of A - dam's sin,

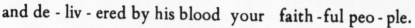

and de - liv - ered by his blood your faith -ful peo - ple.

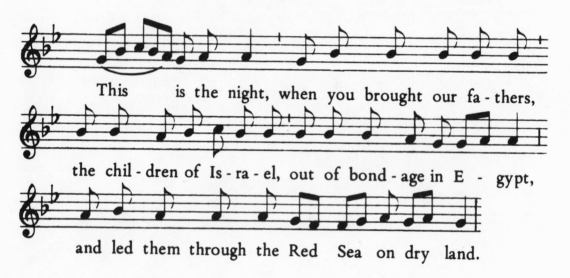

This is the night, when you brought our fa - thers,

the chil - dren of Is - ra - el, out of bond - age in E - gypt,

and led them through the Red Sea on dry land.

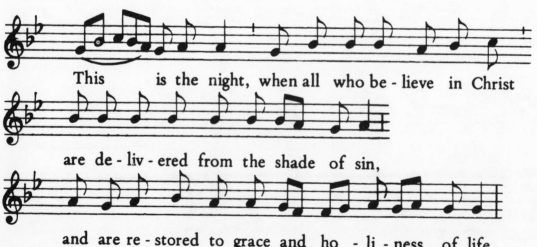

This is the night, when all who be - lieve in Christ

are de - liv - ered from the shade of sin,

and are re - stored to grace and ho - li - ness of life.

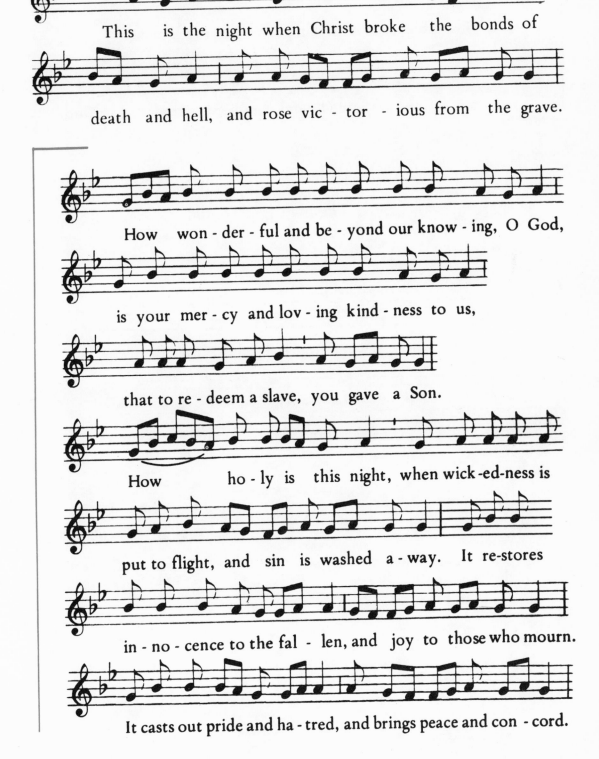

This is the night when Christ broke the bonds of death and hell, and rose vic - tor - ious from the grave.

How won - der - ful and be - yond our know - ing, O God, is your mer - cy and lov - ing kind - ness to us, that to re - deem a slave, you gave a Son.

How ho - ly is this night, when wick -ed-ness is put to flight, and sin is washed a - way. It re-stores in - no - cence to the fal - len, and joy to those who mourn. It casts out pride and ha - tred, and brings peace and con - cord.

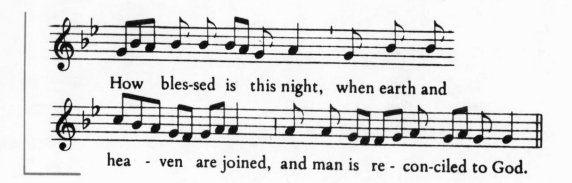

How bles-sed is this night, when earth and

hea - ven are joined, and man is re - con-ciled to God.

If the Paschal Candle was not lit earlier, the Deacon or minister now lights it. From its flame other candles and lamps in the church may be lighted; after which he continues:

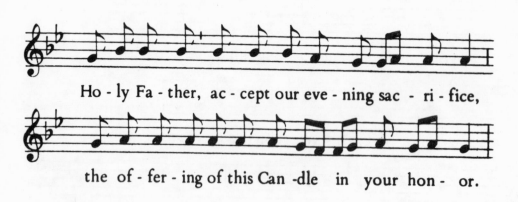

Ho - ly Fa - ther, ac - cept our eve - ning sac - ri - fice,

the of - fer - ing of this Can -dle in your hon - or.

May it shine con - tin-ual-ly to drive a - way all dark-ness.

May Christ, the Morn - ing Star, who knows no set -ting,

find it ev - er burn-ing—

he who gives his light to all cre - a - tion.

We pray you, Lord, to di - rect, sanc - ti - fy, and gov - ern us

your ser - vants, and all your faith - ful fam - i - ly, with

your con-tin - ual grace; that we may pass our time in peace

and glad - ness, in the fes - ti - val of our re - demp -tion;

Through Je - sus Christ your Son our Lord, who lives and

reigns with you in the u - ni - ty of the Ho -ly Spir - it, one God.

for ev - er and ev - er. A - men.

15. We Praise Thee
(*Te Deum laudamus*)

[286]

We praise thee O God;
   we acknowledge thee to be the Lord.
   All the earth doth worship thee, the Father everlasting.
To thee all Angels cry aloud:
the Heavens and all the Powers therein;
   To thee Cherubim and Seraphim continually do cry,
Holy, Holy, Holy, Lord God of Sabaoth;
   Heaven and earth are full of the Majesty of thy glory.
The glorious company of the Apostles praise thee.
   The goodly fellowship of the Prophets praise thee.
The noble army of Martyrs praise thee.
   The holy Church throughout all the world
   doth acknowledge thee;
The Father of an infinite Majesty;
Thine adorable, true, and only Son;
   Also the Holy Ghost the Comforter.

Thou art the King of Glory, O Christ.
   Thou art the everlasting Son of the Father.
When thou tookest upon thee to deliver man,
   thou didst humble thyself to be born of a Virgin.
When thou hadst overcome the sharpness of death,
   thou didst open the Kingdom of Heaven to all believers.
Thou sittest at the right hand of God,
   in the glory of the Father.
We believe that thou shalt come to be our Judge.
   We therefore pray thee, help thy servants,
   whom thou hast redeemed with thy precious blood.
Make them to be numbered with thy Saints,
   in glory everlasting.

[287] ## 16. You Are God
(*Te Deum laudamus*)

You are God: we praise you;
You are the Lord: we acclaim you;
You are the eternal Father:
All creation worships you.
To you all angels, all the powers of heaven,
Cherubim and Seraphim, sing in endless praise:
    Holy, holy, holy Lord, God of power and might,
    heaven and earth are full of your glory.
The glorious company of apostles praise you.
The noble fellowship of prophets praise you.
The white-robed army of martyrs praise you.
Throughout the world the holy Church acclaims you:
    Father, of majesty unbounded,
    your true and only Son, worthy of all worship,
    and the Holy Spirit, Advocate and Guide.

You, Christ, are the king of glory,
eternal Son of the Father.
When you became man to set us free
you did not disdain the Virgin's womb.
You overcame the sting of death
and opened the Kingdom of heaven to all believers.
You are seated at God's right hand in glory.
We believe that you will come and be our judge.
    Come then, Lord, sustain your people,
    bought with the price of your own blood,
    and bring us with your saints
    to everlasting glory.

20. Christ Our Passover

[290]

Christ our Passover is sacrificed for us:
    therefore let us keep the feast,
Not with old leaven,
neither with the leaven of malice and wickedness;
    but with the unleavened bread of sincerity and truth.

Christ being raised from the dead dieth no more;
    death hath no more dominion over him.
For in that he died, he died unto sin once:
    but in that he liveth, he liveth unto God.
Likewise reckon ye also yourselves
to be dead indeed unto sin,
    but alive unto God through Jesus Christ our Lord.

Christ is risen from the dead,
    and become the first fruits of them that slept.
For since by man came death,
    by man came also the resurrection of the dead.
For as in Adam all die,
    even so in Christ shall all be made alive.

[291] ## 21. Christ Our Passover

Alleluia. Alleluia.
Christ our Passover has been sacrificed for us;
    therefore let us celebrate the feast,
Not with the old leaven, the leaven of malice and evil,
    but with the unleavened bread of sincerity and truth.
                                            Alleluia.

Christ being raised from the dead will never die again;
    death no longer has dominion over him.
The death that he died, he died to sin, once for all;
    but the life he lives, he lives to God.
So also consider yourselves dead to sin,
    and alive to God in Jesus Christ our Lord. Alleluia.

Christ has been raised from the dead,
    the first fruits of those who have fallen asleep.
For since by a man came death,
    by a man has come also the resurrection of the dead.
For as in Adam all die,
    so also in Christ shall all be made alive. Alleluia.

Additional Directions and Suggestions

[124] # ADDITIONAL DIRECTIONS AND SUGGESTIONS

The Holy Table is spread with a clean white cloth during the celebration.

A Psalm, or part of a Psalm, may be sung or said at the places indicated in the Services. The addition of Gloria Patri is optional.

On occasion, and when appropriate, instrumental music may be used in place of a Psalm, Hymn, or Anthem.

The Beginning of the Service

When the Litany is sung or said immediately before the Eucharist, the Prayer of Intercession may be omitted. The Litany may be concluded with the Kyries, in which case the Eucharist begins with the Salutation and Collect of the Day.

In the First Service, the Priest may preface the Collect for Purity with an Opening Sentence from Morning or Evening Prayer.

The Decalogue (page 30) with its responses may be used before the Summary of the Law and Kyries, or in place of them.

The Kyrie eleison, or "Lord, have mercy", may be sung or said in three-fold, six-fold, or nine-fold form. The Trisagion, "Holy God", may be sung or said three times.

Gloria in excelsis is sung or said from Christmas Day through the Feast of the Epiphany; on Sundays from Easter Day through the Day of Pentecost, and on Ascension Day; and at other times as desired; but it is not used on the Sundays or ordinary weekdays of Advent or Lent. Te Deum laudamus is not used on the Sundays or ordinary weekdays of Lent.

The Collect of the Day is said by the Bishop or Priest presiding at the celebration. With few exceptions, there is only one Collect at this point. [125]

Concerning the Lessons

It is desirable that the Lessons which precede the Gospel be read from a lectern.

Lessons are announced in the following manner:
"A Reading from [*Name of Book*]",
or "The Word of God, written in [*Name of Book*]",
(A citation in the following words may be added:
  "chapter _____ , beginning at the _____ verse.")

After each Lesson, the reader may say,
"Here ends the Lesson (Reading, Epistle)."

It is desirable that the Gospel be read from the pulpit or a lectern or from the midst of the Congregation.

When a significant portion of the Congregation is composed of persons whose native tongue is other than English, the Gospel may be read in that language by a reader appointed by the Priest, either in place of, or in addition to, the Gospel in English.

A Hymn may be sung before or after the Sermon.

The Nicene Creed may be omitted, except on Sundays and major Feasts.

Directions concerning the Prayer of Intercession will be found on page 111.

The Confession of Sin

A confession of sin is a normal part of the Service, but may be omitted on appropriate occasions. It may be said before

[126] the Liturgy begins; or before or after the Prayer of Intercession. When a confession is used, the Peace should not precede it. When the Confession is omitted, a form of Intercession containing a penitential petition should be chosen.

When there is no Communion

If there is no Communion, all that is appointed through the Prayer of Intercession may be said. (The Confession of Sin under such circumstances should be said before the Service begins or before the Intercession). A Hymn or Anthem may then be sung, and the offerings of the People received. The Service may then conclude with the Lord's Prayer; and with either the Grace or a Blessing, or with the exchange of the Peace.

In the absence of a priest, all that is described above (except for the Absolution and Blessing) may be said by a deacon, or if there is no deacon, by a lay-reader specially licensed by the Bishop.

At the Peace and Offertory

The greeting, "The Peace of the Lord be always with you", is addressed to the entire assembly. In the exchange between individuals which may follow, any appropriate words of greeting may be used.

The greeting of Peace may take place:
1. Before the Offertory Sentence.
2. Before the Prayer of Intercession.
3. Before the ministration of the Sacrament (before or after the Sentence of Invitation.)

Necessary announcements may be made after the Creed, or before the Offertory (before or after the Peace), or at the end of the Service, as convenient.

It is appropriate that the Deacon and other assisting ministers make ready the Table for the celebration, preparing and placing upon it the bread and cup of.wine. (In preparing the [127] chalice it is customary to add a little water.)

Alternative Acclamations at the Great Thanksgiving

One of the following alternative acclamations may be used in the course of the Great Thanksgiving:

A. We remember his death;
    We proclaim his resurrection;
    We await his coming in glory.

B. When we eat this Bread and drink this Cup,
    we proclaim your death, Lord Christ,
    until you come in glory.

At the Breaking of the Bread

At the Breaking of the Bread, in place of "Christ our Passover", some other appropriate Anthem may be used.

If the number of communicants requires the use of additional chalices, it is convenient that Wine which had been consecrated in a flagon be poured into them at the time of the Breaking of the Bread.

At the Ministration of the Sacrament

In the First Service, at the ministration of the Sacrament, the following procedure may be used:

1. Before receiving Communion himself, the Priest says to the People:

    The Body and Blood of our Lord Jesus Christ, given for you, preserve your bodies and souls unto everlasting life. Take this in remembrance that Christ died for you, and feed on him in your hearts by faith, with thanksgiving.

2. The Gifts are then ministered with these words:

    The Body [Blood] of our Lord Jesus Christ. (*Amen.*)

[128]   or he may use this Invitation:

> The Gifts of God for the People of God.

or this Invitation:

> The Gifts of God for the People of God: Take them in remembrance that Christ gives himself for you, and feed on him in your hearts by faith, with thanksgiving.

While the People are coming forward to receive Communion, the presiding Minister receives the Sacrament in both kinds. The bishops, priests, and deacons at the ·Holy Table then communicate, and after them the People.

Opportunity shall always be given to every communicant to receive the consecrated Bread and Wine separately. But the Sacrament may be received in both kinds simultaneously, in a manner approved by the Bishop.

When the presiding Minister is assisted by a deacon or another priest, it is customary for the President to minister the consecrated Bread and the assistant the Chalice. When several deacons or priests are present, some may minister the Bread, others the Wine, as the President may appoint.

The Consecration of Additional Elements

If the Consecrated Bread or Wine does not suffice for the number of communicants, the Priest is to consecrate more of either or both, saying,

> HEAR US, O HEAVENLY FATHER, AND WITH THY (YOUR) WORD AND HOLY SPIRIT BLESS AND SANCTIFY THIS BREAD [WINE] THAT IT, ALSO, MAY BE THE SACRAMENT OF THE PRECIOUS BODY [BLOOD] OF THY (YOUR)SON JESUS CHRIST OUR LORD, WHO TOOK BREAD [THE CUP] AND SAID, "THIS IS MY BODY [BLOOD]". *Amen.*

or else he may consecrate more of both kinds, saying again the Prayer of Consecration, beginning with the words which follow the Sanctus, and ending with the Invocation.

The Ministration of Communion by a Deacon

When there is no priest available, a deacon may be appointed to distribute Holy Communion from the reserved Sacrament in the following manner:

> After the Intercession (and the receiving of the People's offerings), the Deacon reverently places the holy Sacrament on the altar.
>
> The Lord's Prayer is then said, the Deacon first saying, "Let us pray in the words which our Savior Christ has (*hath*) taught us."
>
> And then, omitting the breaking of the Bread, he proceeds with what follows in the Liturgy (page 23 or 57) as far as the end of the Prayer after Communion, after which he dismisses the People.

The Conclusion of the Service

If any of the consecrated Bread or Wine remain, apart from any which may be required for the Communion of the sick or of others who for weighty cause could not be present at the celebration, the Priest (or Deacon) and other communicants shall reverently eat and drink the same, either immediately after the Communion of the People or after the Dismissal.

A hymn of praise may be sung before or after the Prayer after Communion.

From Easter Day through the Day of Pentecost, Alleluia may be added to any of the Dismissals in the following manner:

"Go in peace to love and serve the Lord. Alleluia, alleluia. *Thanks be to God. Alleluia, alleluia.*"

[130]   *The Music of the Liturgy*

In the Second Service, the texts of the Kyrie eleison, Gloria in excelsis, Nicene Creed, and Sanctus given in the Book of Common Prayer may be substituted for the ICET versions when a musical setting composed for the Prayer Book wording is being used.

Musicians are encouraged to write new music for the Services, and especially for the ICET and other new texts.